Beloved as We Are

Building a Congregational Culture of Disability Inclusion

Barbara F. Meyers and Shelly Rohe

Skinner House Books
Boston

Copyright © 2026 by Barbara F. Meyers and Shelly Rohe. All rights reserved.
Published by Skinner House Books, an imprint of the Unitarian Universalist Association, 24 Farnsworth St., Boston, MA 02210–1409.

skinnerhouse.org

Printed in the United States

Cover design by Alex Camlin
Text design by Tim Holtz

print ISBN: 978-1-55896-986-5
eBook ISBN: 978-1-55896-987-2

6 5 4 3 2 1
30 29 28 27 26
Cataloging-in-Publication data on file with the Library of Congress.

Dedicated to disabled Unitarian Universalists and their allies.

Contents

Preface

The impetus for the book is the recent ending of the UUA's Accessibility and Inclusion Ministry (AIM) certification program for congregations, a joint venture between EqUUal Access and the Unitarian Universalist Association (UUA). EqUUal Access is an organization of disabled Unitarian Universalists, together with their families, friends, and allies. The AIM program invited congregations to thoroughly assess what they were doing to enable disabled people to have access to, and be included in, congregational life. Becoming AIM-certified required a multiyear effort led by a dedicated team that worked with congregational leaders and members. Congregations that engaged with this program saw a beautiful culture change that led to greater access and inclusion. However, less than 1 percent of UU congregations were able to put forth this effort. After seven years the program was ended because of this lack of participation, and because we wanted to find different ways to improve the experiences of disabled Unitarians Universalists in their congregations. This book is part of that strategy.

Despite its difficulties, much wisdom was gained by everyone involved in the experience—the congregations that engaged in the program, even the ones that didn't complete it, and what we learned in developing and administering the program. This book is an effort to make this wisdom available to all UU congregations. We hope that they will find it easier to engage with than the more onerous AIM program. Our goal is to dismantle the attitudes and behaviors that not only harm disabled people directly but also keep our congregations from being inclusive and welcoming to all, disabled and nondisabled alike.

A Note on Language

The way we talk about disability gives it life and shapes our impressions about disability into reality. If we talk about disability negatively, it perpetuates the stigma of disability and disabled people being "other." When we use language that makes disability childlike, it infantilizes disabled people and they may not be thought of as serious people. When we try to soften disability or "make it sound better," we perpetuate the idea that disabled people need to be treated with kid gloves or are supposed to be inspirational. The authors of this book intend to treat disability matter-of-factly. Disabled people are part of the fabric of human life.

There are differing opinions about the language that should be used to talk about disability. There will be a section later in this book (page 23) dedicated to language and how it shapes our perception of disability.

Person-first or identity-first language are the two types of language styles most often used when discussing disability. Both were developed to be respectful of this subject. Person-first language is vital for some people when discussing disability. This is where the person comes before their disability, such as, "I am a person with vision loss." Sheri Thomas says, "As a writer, author, disability advocate, and most importantly, as someone who was born with cerebral palsy, I always use person-first language when describing myself or other people with disabilities."

The other style, identity-first language, is where the disability is a descriptor of the person. An example of this type of language is "I'm a disabled person," or "I'm an autistic person." People who use identity-first language recognize disability as an integral part of who they are and don't separate out their diagnosis. The authors of the book will be using identity–first language. For Shelly Rohe, "I am disabled and proud! No one is going to surprise or shock me by telling me that I have a disability. And nobody needs to soften it for me. I'm simply disabled."

We do not use derogatory phrases such as "wheelchair-bound," "the disabled," or "suffering from." Language can change and morph into something new. Words that were once thought of as offensive may come back into favor with different connotations. Communities of people often agree to claim the words they use to define themselves. When it comes to person-first or identity-first language, there is no right or wrong, it is a personal choice. The most respectful thing you can do is to use what the person prefers. If you are speaking to someone, ask the person what they prefer. If you do not have a disability and are writing about the subject, it is often suggested to use person-first language. This book is written by and for disabled Unitarian Universalists. We understand that words used today may change and how we have said things may sound awkward or difficult in the future. For now, we hope this book will help stir conversations and open hearts and minds.

Introduction

This book is motivated by stories, the stories that disabled Unitarian Universalists have been telling for many years to leaders in our movement and congregations, to their fellow congregants, and most recently to us in response to our invitation. These stories have often not been heeded or acted upon, and have sometimes been dismissed as unimportant or too difficult to meaningfully respond to.

The message we want to convey to our beloved movement and to all Unitarian Universalists is this: Heeding and acting on these stories thoughtfully, meaningfully, intentionally, urgently, and in partnership with disabled people is crucial to being who we say we are as Unitarian Universalists, to our individual spiritual vitality, and to that of our congregations. Disabled people are telling us that they are frequently unable to access our buildings and events, participate fully, feel a sense of belonging, or enjoy the spiritual benefits of our faith communities. Accommodations for disabled people are either insufficient or completely absent, their requests are dismissed or even mocked, and negative attitudes about disability are harming them. This is happening in the very places that are supposed to support and nurture them. This is unacceptable in a faith that proclaims love as its paramount value.

And yet there are other stories as well, stories that show how a faith community can uplift disabled people, help them heal from trauma, appreciate and nurture their gifts, support them, and value their presence. We must heed these stories as well. They show what is possible and the difference a full, loving, enthusiastic welcome can make in the lives of people and communities.

We want to emphasize that our project is to promote both accessibility and inclusivity in Unitarian Universalist congregations. Accessibility alone isn't enough; disabled people in accessible spaces and communities may still face physical or social isolation, encounter both micro- and macroaggressions, and be denied leadership opportunities. They may be ignored or treated as inconsequential or irrelevant. We want disabled people to be able not just to be present, not even just to participate, but to fully belong, to thrive. It's also important to note that accessibility and inclusivity involve more than the physical buildings and grounds of a congregation and its use of assistive technologies. They also encompass communications, transportation, food and drink, representation, language, worship style, pastoral care, and socializing. Increasing the inclusion of disabled people in congregational life means recognizing disability as an integral part of the human experience. It means remembering that the worth and dignity of all people is a fundamental principle of our faith.

We can't offer a one-size-fits-all approach to meeting the needs of disabled people. An important part of our message is the importance of engaging with the disabled people in your community to find out what they specifically want and need. We recognize that it is complex and daunting to try to meet everyone's needs, especially when those needs may be in conflict with each other, and we acknowledge that much of the advice that is offered in this book (and elsewhere) about resisting ableism can seem contradictory unless you engage with nuance. We will address these dilemmas with the hope that you will finish reading this book feeling more confident that you can take on the important work of helping your community live out its values, empower disabled people, and make them feel at home.

We do not rely heavily on academic resources in this book; rather we focus on what can be learned from lived experience. It is through lived experience that we all weave our stories into the web that connects us all and makes up the fabric of life. We therefore began by issuing a broad appeal for stories of disability in Unitarian Universalist congregational life, reaching out especially to multiple identity groups, hoping for as much variety of experience as we could get. This is how we phrased our invitation:

> We are seeking authors, named or anonymous, who would be willing to share their authentic story. We want the book to have a strong intersectional framework, so we are looking for stories in which authors bring their whole selves. We welcome you to reflect on how your other identities are part of your experience as a disabled person in a UU community. This book is meant to give insight into how disabled people worship and experience life in their congregations, how disability impacts a person's faith, spiritual identity, and showing up with your authentic self.

One of the first responses we received was from Catherine Olson, who pointed out that many disabled people spend most of their energy just getting through the day. Catherine brings up a very good point; many stories are not represented in this book. There are many reasons for these absences:

- As Catherine says, some people simply don't have the time or energy to spare to compose and share their stories.

- We are missing the stories of people who aren't able to tell their stories orally or in writing. Some disabilities make it very difficult to communicate. Sometimes care partners can help tell these stories, but often there are too many demands on their own time and energy.
- We are missing the stories of people who are not comfortable telling them publicly, even anonymously. They may fear being stigmatized, or losing fellowship and opportunities, if their disability becomes known.
- Too many people in our congregations know the pain of sharing their experiences only to have them dismissed or met with hostility. They may choose not to risk experiencing that again.
- People who have been traumatized by their experiences may not be willing to relive them for our book.

We deeply honor the silence of these voices, knowing we have not captured the whole truth of how disabled people experience Unitarian Universalist congregational life.

It is our intention to present disability as commonplace in every single Unitarian Universalist community. If you believe that there aren't enough disabled people in your community to justify a concerted effort to assess what accommodations are needed and implement them, and to take a hard look at what may be making it difficult for some members to participate in community life, then we can guarantee you that a significant number of your people are being left out of the full experience of congregational life, and they are being harmed by that.

We recognize that our readers are both disabled and nondisabled and that we will be discussing some painful stories. We do not want to cause harm. If you have a trauma response to anything in this book, please put it down and take care of yourself. But if you are feeling defensive and resistant, we ask you to open your heart and keep reading, recognizing that disabled people often have no choice but to stay at the table when things get uncomfortable.

Every Congregation Has Work to Do

As you begin reading this book, you may feel that your congregation is pretty good at including disabled people. Perhaps you think you don't have many disabled people in your congregation anyway, and their needs are being adequately met. Perhaps you have done everything that they've asked you for, or that the Americans with Disabilities Act demands, or at least everything that you think is reasonable or practical. We will address the latter points in various ways throughout the rest of this book, but in this chapter we'd like to focus on whether you truly know who the disabled people in your community are and what they need.

Many disabilities are not easily discernible to observers. Collectively, we became more aware of this during the COVID-19 pandemic, when "underlying health conditions" became a common phrase in the daily news. Conditions that are not apparent to others but that significantly impact a person's life have always been prevalent in our congregations, just as they are everywhere. They may be characterized primarily by illness, pain, fatigue, a weak immune system, neurodiversity, mental health challenges, or environmental sensitivities. They may be progressive, intermittent, or situational. The people experiencing them may mask or manage their effects or avoid certain situations or activities when they can't; they may do this so thoroughly that others don't see the effort the disabled person is making.

Even if a perfect understanding of the needs of disabled people in your congregation were possible, it would only be a snapshot of those needs at a particular moment. Nearly everyone will be disabled at some point in their lives. Progressive diseases intensify over time. Nondisabled people get sick or injured, becoming disabled either temporarily or permanently. Anyone who lives into old age will experience some sort of disability as a natural part of the aging process. As Dana Snyder-Grant told us, "Issues of aging and disability can overlap with each other as we experience loss, wisdom, and perspective. Our collective liberation means that we are all on this journey together." Pey Carter pointed out, "The likelihood that a person will move on with perfect health is almost impossible. Some just have illnesses sooner than others."

Rev. Bob Murphy: Old folks are often resented, attacked, scammed, and segregated, because of their age. Ageism is often explicit and unquestioned, on both the political left and the political right. Disability rights advocates understand the situation. Everybody, without exception, should look forward to aging.

Helen Armstrong: Part of my hope for our faith is based on continuity and the journey together through different life stages. I am now grappling with becoming an elder. For most of us, eldership means embracing the twists and turns of illness and disability. Our congregations can do more to help us adapt to and celebrate different life stages and incorporate a celebration of disability wholeness. Let's build on the collective care work we already offer to those congregants who face a sudden life crisis. Remember that as many of us move forward toward eldership, we are all going to join the disabled path sooner or later. Let's embrace this rich journey, show our whole selves more, and do it together.

Diana C. Archibald: Right now, I am disabled and not disabled. I have Parkinson's disease. Strangers look at me, and even if they notice my tremor, they don't interpret it as Parkinson's or tag me as a disabled person. People who have known me for a long time, like my closest friends at the UU church where my husband and I belong, may see enough of a change to consider placing me in that category. However, most people can't tell where I am on the spectrum of disability. Then again, neither can I.

What nobody sees is the constipation, incontinence, dry mouth, morning nausea, foot and hand pain, muscle soreness, random pricks on my skin, insomnia, et cetera. They don't see my evening anxiety surges, my trouble keeping track of time, or my compulsion to finish tasks even if it means staying up all night.

I know there's no cure for Parkinson's. One day there will be no question about whether I am disabled. Will I have a church community that's there for me when that happens? And what role can I play meanwhile in the life of the church?

Honestly, it's hard for me to see a future at our church. At least, it's hard to imagine going into the building for programming. So what does church look like for me going forward? I don't know.

And what about the disabled people you may never get to know because they find the congregation inaccessible, or who arrive and quickly leave again because of the barriers they face to full participation?

Anonymous: Our building does not have a ramp or any way for a person using a wheelchair to get in. I'm lucky that I can walk, but I know plenty of people who would like to attend our services and can't get in the building. I've got my own barriers because of my eyesight. There are plenty of times I wish I could use a ramp because I don't want to stumble up the steps. There are no handrails and unless someone is there, I'm afraid I'll fall every time.

It is always worthwhile to knock down barriers to full inclusion for even one disabled person, but it's also worth considering that every accommodation, even if meant for only one person, is probably also making your congregation feel more like home for others who have different disabilities, are disabled without the congregation knowing, or may become beloved members in the future.

DISABILITY BASICS

Let's begin with some basic information about disabilities and the disability community. Educating yourself is an important first step in building a congregational culture of inclusion. Knowing this context will help you feel comfortable and respond with more confidence when disabled people share with you what they need and how they're feeling, and your familiarity with these concepts and with some common experiences of disabled people will help them to trust that you care enough to have made the effort to learn.

Non-Apparent Disabilities

Unfortunately, people with non-apparent disabilities who ask for accommodations are often met with skepticism from those who assume they are exaggerating or faking their needs. This lack of understanding can create barriers to access and equity and leave the disabled person feeling isolated or invalidated. It is important to have empathy and an open mind and not to make assumptions based on appearances. Trusting that people are the best judges of their own needs creates a more inclusive and supportive environment, where everyone can participate fully without the need to constantly justify or explain their circumstances.

Rev. Jennifer DeBusk Alviar: The world of neurodiversity is nuanced, often invisible. I am a white, able-bodied, cisgender woman who presents as nondisabled. My non-apparent disabilities relate to executive functioning around word finding, information processing, and memory recall. What cannot be seen is frequently dismissed as invalid. After all, where is the proof? Where is the evidence?

Yet it is my lived experience as a disabled minister that brings credibility and integrity to my vocation, not in spite of it. My cognitive challenges are the very impetus for shaping a more inclusive, embodied, multisensory approach to faith that benefits disabled and non-disabled people alike. These are the "invisible" connections that our society misses in its quest for proof-based evidence.

Dana Snyder-Grant: I've had multiple sclerosis for forty-two years, all my adult life. I have flare-ups of double vision or leg weakness and spasticity or decreased coordination in my hands, often accompanied by excessive fatigue. If, prior to the MS, I had difficulty asking for help, trusting my own judgment, or accepting limitations, these struggles would surely come back to haunt me. Since the MS was mostly invisible, I was able to integrate well into the congregation with one exception: the pulpit area up front required stairs and there was no railing. To get up there, I needed to go around the back and come in a different way. I felt different from everyone else, and I felt excluded.

Helen Armstrong: In December 2023, I moved from moderately to severely disabled when I acquired Long COVID. Suddenly the disabilities I sought to hide from my UU contacts became much more pronounced. For over a year, I showed up at Sunday service in a scooter, which I hid in a hallway. People frequently asked how I was doing and I found it exhausting to try to answer. I began to improve after eighteen months and was peppered on Sunday mornings with comments about how well I was doing. It felt like I was supposed to rejoin the ranks of the able bodied and reinstate normalcy. I found no space to be listened to by nondisabled congregants about my ongoing struggles. One congregant told me that I was not yet recovered because I had not learned the lesson that I needed. I was shocked with his display of ableism. Long COVID had not gone away and I was dealing with constant grief about my many limitations. UU friends who had reached out in the first 18 months began to drift back into their own lives. I tried to keep up but found I had to do most of the reaching out, and this became increasingly difficult and wearying.

In my first year of Long COVID, I helped established a congregational Accessibility Committee, and we got a mask-only section instituted in the sanctuary. It was far off in a corner and my partner and I were typically the only ones who sat there. Most people huddled in the middle section, which felt unsafe to me. I found it hard to participate in coffee time in a crowded and noisy coffee space where almost no one masked. I helped bring in a disability justice speaker, but this felt like a one-off event with no follow up. Ableism permeates the space to this day.

I wish to be around UUs who are interested in allyship, specifically learning about disabled lives with curiosity and compassion, not offering advice or dismissive pronouncements. Interest in further exploring ableism as an oppression and how it intersects with other "isms" would go a long way, especially when strongly supported by allies and not those of us directly impacted by the oppression.

A common reason for a disability to be non-apparent is that the disabled person is managing it to make it so. This can require a great deal of effort. They may avoid certain situations or even isolate themselves, perhaps out of embarrassment or fear of social consequences if others notice their disability.

Some people with non-apparent disabilities do not share what is happening with them for fear that they will be rejected, left out, or thought of differently. Some may even have a hard time acknowledging the extent of their condition, which can make it difficult for them even to request, let alone receive, the accommodations or other support they may need.

Sheri Thomas: After being diagnosed with a mental health condition, I began to unpack the realities of the stigma surrounding mental illness—and to discover how much progress needs to be made. In 2014, I was hospitalized and first diagnosed with bipolar disorder. As I struggled to accept the diagnosis, I refused to follow up with psychiatric treatment or take my medication as directed, which led to a much more serious bipolar episode in 2019 that almost cost me my life. After surviving a suicide attempt, I listened to my doctors, took my medication, and, most importantly, accepted my diagnosis. When I was first hospitalized in 2014, however, I was too ashamed to tell anyone that I had a mental health issue. I was afraid to talk about it because I, like so many others, held deeply internalized negative attitudes about mental illness and seeking help.

I was fortunate to get the help I needed, and I hope anyone else struggling will do the same. If I can encourage one person to get help in an emergency by contacting 911 or 988 (the Suicide and Crisis Lifeline) in the U.S. or reaching out to their minister, their church community, a family member, friend, general practitioner, psychiatrist, psychologist, or therapist, my story will have made a difference.

Sometimes a person's condition is apparent to others, but they do not consider it "really" disabling even though the individual with the condition sees themselves as disabled.

Rev. Keith Kron: As someone with severe arthritis in two toes that requires special orthotics and good shoes, almost always running shoes, I know that people over the years have dismissed this as not mattering while others would always tell me how casually I was dressed. Being diabetic as well has been diminished, despite my being continually asked why I don't consume alcohol or indulge in sweets at the potluck after church.

I have been told my conditions aren't disabilities because I manage them. And somehow a disability therefore is something one can't manage. Along with that there is the assumption I manage these on my own, which is not true. Yet therein lies a rub—the belief that self-sufficiency is devoid of community connection and that needing others makes one insufficient, at least for some things.

People with non-apparent disabilities can also have a harder time finding their place in the disabled community. They may feel like impostors for claiming the label of "disabled" even when their conditions significantly impact their lives. When their community expects them to function as if they don't have disabilities, they may find themselves unable to fully participate, left out of the disabled community's support system, and isolated.

Keith Kron: It was only a few years ago that the UUA as an institution offered up an affinity group for staff members with a disability. I tentatively showed up, buying into a notion that I really wouldn't be welcome there or shouldn't even be there. Yet I was asked to facilitate the group, arranging meetings, assuring confidentiality, and creating a space where people can show up and be themselves wholly and fully. It's been an honor. And one of the favorite hours of each month.

Rev. Amanda Schuber: Identity matters. It defines how we move through and experience the world. It's core to our relationships and our connections. Far too often, as a person living with a hidden disability, I'm relegated to the fringes of community, trying not to take up too much space and unsure where I fit in.

Progressive Disabilities

People with a disability that is gradually progressing are especially in need of a supportive community. They need to know that as their disability intensifies, they will still be known, loved, and included, that they will be supported, that they will still be able to contribute to their community, and that their contributions will be valued.

As they work to come to terms with their changing experience, they are often dealing with intense and complex emotions, including fear. Unfortunately, fear of both how their disability may progress and how the attitudes and behavior of others toward them may change can lead them to deny what's happening or even to withdraw from community just when they need it most.

Kaden Colton: I struggled to admit that I was losing my vision to others, especially in new situations like attending church. I found it challenging to deal with the cultural taboo of disability and, in particular, blindness. I didn't know how to deal with situations where I couldn't see something or adjust to learning how to recognize people by voice and the features I could see.

Diana C. Archibald: From 2000 to 2015, I became very involved in the church, teaching religious education classes for children, leading the Green Sanctuary certification effort, chairing the mission statement revision committee, starting a women's group, volunteering for events, and contributing time and treasure as I was able. Our child was also very involved in church activities, especially when we ended up home-schooling from eighth grade through high school. The church became a crucial part of her education and a lifeline for me at a busy and stressful time of my life as I was trying to advance my career as a professor. Both on campus and at church, I was a face that people recognized, a name that people knew, a valued member of a community.

Then things fell apart. Nearly three years and three medical opinions after my symptoms started, I learned that I have Parkinson's disease. I did not fully believe it, but this time I could not shrug it off. I grieved, I cried, I dove into exercise, I cleared the deck of all the things I didn't want to do anymore, didn't have time to do, because I was fighting for my life, it seemed.

I just could not believe this was really happening in the prime of my life—just when I was promoted to full professor, serving as associate chair of my department and training to be chair, becoming known as an established scholar in my field, and, to top it all off, just when my parenting responsibilities had been greatly reduced. The dissonance was hard to bear. I began to hide my symptoms. I wasn't sure what people would think if they knew I had this disease. Would they assume that I was mentally incompetent as well as physically disabled? So I would sit on my right hand to hide the tremor, or hold something in that hand to hide the clenching. The charade was exhausting.

I began to withdraw from people. I sat on a rocking chair on our front porch and stared at the trees.

In the fall of 2017, I finally stood up in church to tell my secret. I approached the stand where we light candles of joy and concern, and with a trembling hand, I tried to light my candle but had to pass it to the volunteer at the stand to light for me. My tremor is always worse when I feel emotional, and it was quite visible at that moment. "I have been diagnosed with Parkinson's disease. There's no cure. But I'm doing fine at this point, and it is a slow progression because I am younger." To be honest, I don't remember what I said. I think I cried a little. No, I didn't let myself cry or I wouldn't have been able to get through it.

Masking

Communities really exacerbate internalized ableism when they subtly or overtly pressure disabled members to mask their disabilities. Masking means acting as if their disabilities don't exist, pushing themselves, in spite of pain, illness, or limited capacity, to contribute in the same ways that nondisabled people can. No one should ever feel that they have to mask to be accepted. Acceptance is only authentic if it fosters true inclusion and supports people's overall well-being. Masking a disability creates a sense of hiding and dishonesty, even if the masking is in a sense encouraged by the congregation.

Rev. Keith Kron: Starting in 2010, when I became the UUA's transitions director, overseeing ministerial placement, more and more ministerial colleagues began to share their own disability stories with me, including their own experiences with mental health issues.

It became clear to me that the closet was huge. As I began to have more of these conversations, I estimated that about a quarter of our ministers identified as having some disability and hid or strongly downplayed their conditions out of fear that they would be considered unemployable. (In 2011, a search committee decided against a minister explicitly because the minister had disclosed being in therapy.)

A few colleagues began to wonder how to be authentic, if they could. Many chose not to disclose. A few did. I suggested that ministers of all identities present themselves beyond a single story. So often ministers have been reduced to a single story. And if they were known for a disability, that became their remembered story.

Rev. Amanda Schuber: While passing does give me the space to blend in, it also frequently blurs my identity in ways that make me, as a person, invisible in my lived experience.

Someone who is masking may push themselves further than they can comfortably or even safely go, for the sake of fitting in. This can exacerbate the very symptoms they are trying to conceal.

Rev. Amanda Schuber: My desire to fit in meant that I would remain quiet, walk the five blocks to the restaurant with the rest of my colleagues, and silently tolerate the searing pain that would tear through my body. Those compromises were easier than trying to justify the accommodations I knew I needed, despite not outwardly appearing to. It was, and remains now more than twenty years later, difficult for people to see me as anything other than able-bodied. Most would describe me as bubbly, full of energy, and bursting with life, and they wouldn't be wrong, but what they don't see is the constant and exhausting internal struggle that passing costs.

Disabled people who are masking have no accommodations or support as they struggle to move and behave like nondisabled people, and they may be judged by standards that are not appropriate for them.

Kelly Riedesel: I did feel a lot of pressure when my son was younger to volunteer in religious education. It was difficult to commit to those things. I was going through the process of applying for disability. I was having a lot of scary surgeries. My mother started to need a lot of my help. My husband was in a difficult job that was draining. It was stressful in my household. It was hard to say no to helping in RE because there were expectations that the parents would be teachers and mentors, which I generally agreed with. It was something I struggled with because I'm naturally a responsible person and I had not figured out an effective way to say no to things back then.

One thing that was particularly difficult for me was when I was teaching religious education. There was an autistic child in my class, and I knew that, but I didn't really know him, and I didn't know how his situation might present itself. I was already struggling just to physically be there and be the person in charge. He did have some conflict one day with the other kids in the class, and the RE director needed to come in to help resolve the situation. I felt ashamed that I didn't know how to help the kids better. I wasn't in a place yet to describe myself as disabled to anyone. I didn't know how to communicate my own struggles, so when the conflict arose with the kids, I realized I hadn't explained to her how unsure I had been feeling about taking on a classful of children. I can look back now and see how better communication and understanding would have helped all the way around.

What I want people to understand about my disability is that I have to learn to discern what's worth doing despite how I'm feeling. So if I'm present at church or anywhere in public, it's because I'm choosing (very carefully) to do that despite probably not feeling very well.

Rev. Katie Norris: I did not know how to live out my faith because there were a lot of expectations to being a good UU that I could not meet. If I don't volunteer for certain types of church events, such as staying overnight to host families in need, am I then not focused enough on social justice? Is it disruptive to have time agnosia and sometimes be late for meetings? What if I need the agenda printed out on paper when we have gone paperless for environmental reasons? I did not know what to do, so I just made sure that at church I masked really well.

Sometimes it's hard to perceive that a disabled person is in pain or sick or fatigued, not because they're deliberately masking but because they aren't sure how to raise the subject. They may be concerned about the effect that doing so might have on the immediate conversation, or on their overall relationship with the person they're talking to. In general, it's better to trust that people, whether you know they are disabled or not, are doing what they can, how they can, and not make any assumptions about their well-being or capacities in any given moment. People should not have to constantly disclose disability in order to manage others' expectations of them.

Rev. Katie Norris: We build trust, in part, by practicing non-judgment. If you notice someone is always late for board meetings, for example, rather than sending them an email saying that lateness harms the rest of the group and is a disrespect of their time, which is a judgment based on your own or the group's cultural norms, don't attach a moral judgment to the fact of lateness.

Kate Ryan: Although I'm in constant terrible pain, it does not show on my face, and so when people ask me how I am, I am at an impasse. I want to be open about my disabilities, but I don't want to depress people. This is the hardest part about disabilities. This is what we don't tell you. This is what you should know anyway.

On the other hand, people who are unable or unwilling to completely mask their disability are often condemned as "not trying hard enough" to fit in. This judgment arises from and furthers the idea that disability is something to be fixed or hidden. Suggesting that a person must conceal their identity to be accepted perpetuates stigma and refuses to value them for their authentic self. Embracing and respecting disability as part of human diversity helps build a more inclusive and understanding congregation.

The pressure to mask is self-perpetuating. When disabled people allow themselves to be known in the fullness of their identities and life experiences, it helps others to do the same. A congregation that fosters a culture of affirmation is not only supporting the people who are known to have disabilities but also those disabled people who are masking and anyone else who may be afraid to reveal their true self and lived experience. They may be watching and trying to feel out if it's safe to reveal themselves.

Helen Armstrong: I keep returning to my UU congregation, despite frustrations I feel in that space as a person living with non-apparent chronic illness. I still feel the pressure to pass in UU spaces when I feel ill. It can be hard to show myself fully there with our persistent white Protestant patterns that mandate a strong work ethic and the need to present as fine. But like most UUs, I have a yearning for more acceptance and understanding from others, for interdependence and wholeness. My congregation is one of the only spaces holding out promise for me to connect with others and build deeper relationships.

Imari S. Nuyen-Kariotis: I want to bring my whole self to my UU congregation, without having to hide or change who I am. Showing up with your authentic self is important to everyone, but it can be especially challenging for disabled people. We often feel like we have to hide our disabilities in order to be accepted. This can be a difficult and isolating experience. However, it is important to remember that we are not alone. There are many other disabled people who are also struggling to show up with their authentic selves. We need to support each other and to create a space where we can all be ourselves. This means being proud of who we are and not letting our disabilities define us.

Unitarian Universalist congregations have the power to help all people, including disabled people, build the sense of their inherent worth and dignity that enables them to share the whole truth about themselves with the world. They can be safe places to try on a disabled identity and practice advocating for oneself, if we intentionally and mindfully make them so.

Kevin Wilson: For me, Unitarian Universalism is a chosen faith, and the person I was when I came into the faith was very different from the person that I am today. When I first entered the church that would become my new spiritual home, I was afraid and hiding. According to the outside world, I was not disabled because I did not look disabled. I became an expert at hiding my true identity and blending in with the able-bodied world.

The Stigma of Mental and Emotional Disabilities

Mentally and emotionally disabled people often experience a particularly high level of social stigma and isolation as well as internalized ableism. They may be discriminated against, harshly judged, and treated badly in both work and social contexts. In some societies and families, people are discouraged from marrying anyone with even a family history of mental illness.

Rev. Katie Norris: While I was open about having bipolar, PTSD, and ADHD, I also knew that I had to be the "good" kind of person with these brain differences, meaning I'd better not have disruptive or different behavior. I can never have a visible mental health flare, and my family and I can't ever ask for help because then people would know that I was not doing well, which was a huge risk, especially as I started on my path to ministry. For ministers, there is this teaching that we need to be healed in order to minister, and most people interpret being healed as not having any sort of mental health struggles. It's okay to have had depression and talk about it, but not okay to be depressed.

Sheri Thomas: One day I shared with a minister that I had bipolar disorder and they said, "That's fine. You are welcome here. Unless your behavior becomes disruptive, and then we would have a conversation about that." All I said was "Okay." I got the message that it was okay to be me, but not fully me.

Sometimes people have trouble acknowledging that they have mental or emotional problems, either to others or even to themselves. Social stigma can create a negative self-image, and people may fear that anyone who finds out about their condition will shun them. This means that people who need help may hide their symptoms and avoid seeking treatment. So many suffer in silence without revealing the source of the shame they feel.

Shame and stigma can lead to isolation, and isolation only makes the situation worse. A caring community, something that congregations should excel at being, is an important support for people coming to terms with, living with, and even recovering from these kinds of disabilities.

Openly stigmatizing and judging mental and emotional disabilities is devastating to people living with these conditions, but pressure not to talk about them is just as harmful. A community that breaks this silence and provides a safe space for people to share their experiences is creating an opportunity for powerful healing.

Sheri Thomas: Since my time in treatment for bipolar disorder, I have noticed that people seem to have no trouble talking endlessly about our physical health when we get together with family and friends: "I just went to see a new orthopedist." "I just completed a new round of physical therapy." Our health comes up naturally in both serious conversations and small talk. But we don't open up about our mental health in a similarly casual way. You rarely hear someone mentioning that they were just diagnosed with borderline personality disorder or that they're running late for a therapy appointment. This needs to change. If we continue to hide the reality of our mental health, we perpetuate a cycle of stigma and shame. To do my part in dismantling a culture of stigma and silence, I now confidently tell others that I have bipolar disorder or mention that I have an appointment with my psychiatrist.

By normalizing my experience, I hope to play a part in removing the stigma and fear surrounding mental health. My story is evidence of how someone can live and thrive with both a physical disability and a mental health issue. Now I'm comfortable saying, "I have cerebral palsy, I have bipolar disorder, and I'm not alone. Many of us have physical disabilities and mental health issues."

Katherine Rubie: I'm not saying that we must get all wrapped up in the drama of somebody's mental illness or go to extraordinary lengths to change things. What I am suggesting is simple changes. I think our congregation could do more. We could provide occasional sermons and/or brief workshops after services, or even have mental health ministry circles, to help the larger congregation understand various mental illnesses. This would go a long way toward breaking down some of the myths and stereotypes, and thus fears and discomfort, around people with mental health disabilities.

The book *Held: Showing Up for Each Other's Mental Health* by Barbara Meyers illustrates how members of liberal religious congregations can support both those living with mental health problems and their loved ones, in our congregations and in society at large. The book and the UU Mental Health Network (uumentalhealth.org/) offer resources for congregations looking to improve their understanding of mental health.

During the COVID-19 pandemic, mental and emotional health problems surged around the world, and many Unitarian Universalist congregations gained a greater understanding of how these conditions affect people and how they can help. That is progress that we can build upon.

Models of Disability

Society has collectively regarded, defined, and responded to disability in many ways in different times and places. These ways of conceptualizing disability, these models, guide our understanding of what it is and how it impacts people's lives. They influence all aspects of our lives: social and economic policy, healthcare and education, and how communities and subgroups within the larger society interpret and respond to disability within their purview. Different models emphasize different aspects of disability and promote or hinder different ways of assigning meaning to it. When we discuss disability, therefore, it is important to be intentional and clear about which one we are using as our framework.

The two most prominent models of disability are the medical model and the social model. Faith-based and nonprofit organizations may maintain a charity or moral model. There are others as well, such as theological and biopsychological models. We will discuss a few here.

Until the mid-1970s, disability was primarily understood through the medical model. The **medical model** interprets disability as a brokenness that needs to be fixed. It assumes that there exists a "normal" state of being, which an "abnormal" state falls short of, and thus that a disabled person should always be seeking a cure. In this model, the disability is the focus rather than the person. When a disabled person is unable to do the things a nondisabled person can, when they are excluded or isolated, the medical model blames them and their disability, whether physical or mental. It does not value their hopes, dreams, and spiritual goals or recognize their right to inclusion and equal treatment. Instead, it sees people only in terms of their disabilities and makes them individually responsible for accommodating their own needs. The medical model lingers on and still predominates in some circles.

The medical model presents itself as caring, and it can be difficult at first to understand how it can be detrimental. After all, healthcare professionals are supposed to help, or at the least to do no harm. The problem is that it places a disabled person's desires and feelings secondary to the "problem" of disability itself. This model is not endorsed by the UUA or by EqUUal Access.

The **rehabilitation model** is related to the medical model. It focuses on minimizing the impact of disability by bolstering a person's capacity and independence, and on limitations in the person's functionality rather than on possible medical or psychiatric causes of those limitations.[1]

The **charity or tragedy model** of disability, which is also closely related to the medical model, can be summed up by the word *pity*. In this model, the disabled person is regarded as a tragic victim. Like the medical model, it ignores the person, focusing instead on what they "have," and sees disability of any kind as something to be feared and avoided. Disability-focused charities have long used this model to tug at heartstrings and prompt donations; it underpins a whole industry around disability. Where the medical model sees medical professionals as experts in disability, the charity model sees non-disabled people as the saviors of disability and celebrates their generosity toward people who are supposedly dependent on them for care.[2] Numerous nonprofits that exist to support and care for people with a particular type of disability follow the charity model; despite their good intentions and although they may be praiseworthy in many respects, they often end up inappropriately classifying, segregating, and even institutionalizing many disabled people.

Like the medical model of disability, the charity model is not endorsed by the UUA or EqUUal Access. Positioning disabled people as dependent on the charity of others infantilizes them.

If you are considering doing something for a disabled person, it's important to ask yourself, "If our congregation, or the

1 For more on the rehabilitation model, see "Disability Theory," a guide produced by the University Library at the University of Illinois Urbana-Champaign, last updated October 11, 2024, https://guides.library.illinois.edu/c.php?g=549817&p=3774564.

2 Nim Ralph, "Understanding Disability: Part 4—The Charity Model," blog entry, December 20, 2017, drakemusic.org/blog/nim-ralph/understanding-disability-part-4-the-charity-model.

government, were offering appropriate supports to disabled people, would this person still need my help? How can I advocate for those supports to be offered?" Curiosity and open-mindedness are key to overcoming the harmful attitudes that the medical, rehabilitation, and charity models of disability promote.

The **social model** of disability begins with fundamentally different assumptions than these. Under the social model, a disabled person's capacity or functionality is what it is, but it need not necessarily lead to disability. In many cases, disability only arises when social conditions exclude people with certain capacities or functionalities. Closely related to the social model is the **cultural model**, which understands disability as a social construct influenced by societal beliefs and practices, including what is considered "normal" or "abnormal" in a society's culture. Under these models, disabled people are responsible neither for their own disability nor for accommodating it; rather, it is society's responsibility to provide an environment as inclusive and free of barriers as possible. Disability is only "bad" insofar as it causes the disabled person pain or suffering; disabilities are simply part of the fabric of life. In Unitarian Universalist terms, they are strands in the interdependent web of existence, of which we are all a part. The Americans with Disabilities Act (ADA) is an example of this model in action, but unfortunately it does not impose any legal obligation on places of worship.

The social model does not deny the value of wheelchairs, hearing aids, glasses, pain medication, and other supports. It acknowledges that rehabilitative interventions like these can promote emotional well-being and improve functionality and independence, without conceiving of disability or disabled people as something to be "fixed."

The UUA and EqUUal Access support the social model of disability.

The **biopsychosocial model** conceives of disability comprehensively and holistically, from biological, individual, and social perspectives. It integrates the medical and social models. Genetics, physiology, and other biological factors may offer significant information about a person's health condition and inform decisions about treatment. However, personal factors such as age, coping mechanisms, self-sufficiency, and adaptability will influence how a person experiences their condition, as will societal factors such as relationships, cultural norms, access to services and environments, and public policy. The biopsychosocial model has been promoted by the World Health Organization (WHO) and is accepted by many countries. As psychologist Nancy Doyle says, it "allows us to provide therapeutic intervention (medical model) and recommend structural accommodation (legislative obligation) without pathologization (social model). In other words, we can deal pragmatically with the individuals who approach us and strive for the best outcomes, given their profile and environment."

This model is controversial. Disability advocates like Andrew Hogan believe that it has led to the social model being absorbed into the medical model, rather than prompting the medical model to engage with the social model's perspective on disability.[3]

One can find something positive in each model, and sometimes benefits of different ones can be combined. Interpreting disability through a model helps a society determine where to

3 Andrew J. Hogan, "Moving Away from the 'Medical Model': The Development and Revision of the World Health Organization's Classification of Disability," *Bulletin of the History of Medicine* 93, no. 2 (Summer 2019), doi.org/10.1353/bhm.2019.0028.

spend money. (And doesn't it always come down to money?) For example, if a society is using a medical model, it may prioritize spending on medical research. Because this model aims to "fix" or "cure" disability, disabled people are made to feel ashamed. But at the same time, advances in therapies or treatments may reduce their pain or increase their capacities. A society that uses the social model, on the other hand, will spend money on making places more accessible.

Models help us center disability and include more diversity in our congregations and communities. As the Office of Developmental Primary Care at the University of California, San Francisco, puts it, "When we try to remove disability from the human experience, society misses out on all the beautiful and brilliant things our community has to offer."[4]

Disability Identity

The shift, in recent years, from the medical model of disability to the social model is closely connected to the emergence of disability as an identity rather than a set of limitations. Jen Sarché, disabled writer and public health officer, draws the connection:

> Many of us, including those of us with significant functional limitations, communication difficulties and high support needs, strongly identify with our disabilities. They represent important elements of how we see ourselves and how we connect to our families and to the

4 "Medical and Social Models of Disability," Office of Developmental Primary Care, University of California, San Francisco, accessed October 20, 2025, odpc.ucsf.edu/clinical/patient-centered-care/medical-and-social-models-of-disability.

> larger society. We may have lower self-worth when we internalize the belief that a central piece of our personhood is wrong and needs to be fixed.[5]

The disability pride movement celebrates disabled people and culture, cultivates solidarity, and raises awareness of the inequities that disabled people face. Disability Pride Month is celebrated in July to commemorate the passage of the Americans with Disabilities Act in July 1990. You may have seen the ad campaign "Disability Is Not a Dirty Word," highlighting the lives of disabled people who are proud of their disabled identity and encouraging positive associations with the word *disabled*.

Pey Carter: Every year I tell people that July is Disability Pride Month—and every year, I get the same surprised reaction. Most people didn't know it existed. Almost no one knows we even have a flag. One of the reasons, in my opinion, is that people with disabilities are viewed very differently than other oppressed and minority groups.

As a queer disabled person, the transition from LGBTQ+ Pride Month to Disability Pride Month is extremely difficult. In June, you have allies making posts about equal rights, Pride flags are raised, there are parades and festivals, companies promote their LGBTQ-inclusive policies, and there is merchandise covered with the rainbow flag or progress flag in almost every major store. Then we get to July and it's crickets. Allies are quiet. Companies don't promote their policies and efforts to hire people with disabilities. There's no disability pride merch and no increase in visibility of people with disabilities. There are very few festivals or parades celebrating our existence and worth. The sole burden of advocacy work and awareness falls on the

5 Jennifer Sarché, "Embracing Disability Identity Is Empowering for Me," *Psychology Today* (July 30, 2025).

shoulders of disabled people and their loved ones, just the same as the other eleven months in the year. Only this month, the feeling is heavier and it hurts, because it doesn't have to be this way.

Ableist Language

Language is a powerful tool that shapes our perceptions of and interactions with the world around us. The phrases we use, often without a second thought, can carry deep-seated implications and reinforce societal attitudes, including toward disability. Ableist language may reinforce harmful stereotypes of disability, stigmatize disabled people, or exclude them by implicitly assuming that no one, or at least no one relevant, is disabled. Lumping all disabled people together and describing them as though they were an undifferentiated mass is another form of ableist language; it denies the richness and diversity of lived experience and hinders the full inclusion of disabled people in all their variety. The models of disability discussed in the last chapter heavily influence the language we use to refer to disability, and understanding these connections will help us to avoid using language that perpetuates outdated and harmful models and the ideas associated with them. By becoming more aware of the implications of our language, we can work toward dismantling harmful stereotypes and foster a more inclusive dialogue that respects and values all people.

Person-first and identity-first language. Using person-first language, such as "I'm a person with autism" or "She is living with multiple sclerosis," emphasizes the person before their disability and has long been advocated as a way to resist the medical model's tendency to reduce people to their diagnoses.

Alternatively, identity-first language, like "I'm a blind person" or "He's disabled," asserts the disability as an integral part of the person's identity, allowing them to fully embrace their experiences of disability. Consider the word "tall." It is more natural to say "I am a tall person" than "I am a person with tallness." As always, context is important in the choice of phrasing. Members of many disability communities tend to understand their disability as an identity, although this is more common for some disabilities than for others, and in these communities identity-first language is often but not always preferred. In the stories and reflections that are shared in this book, we have preserved the language that people use to describe themselves. Using the word *disabled*, which was long considered impolite, is now considered consistent with the social model because it focuses attention on the disabling constraints that society puts on people with certain conditions that would not otherwise be disabling. It also recognizes that some disabling conditions do in fact limit one's abilities. For example, a person on a limited medical diet due to a gastrointestinal condition is more disabled at a restaurant, where it may be difficult or impossible to find food they won't react to, than at home, where they have full access to the foods they can eat. But no matter where they are or how they're accommodated, the fact remains that they still cannot eat certain foods. Especially for people navigating grief and loss around disabling conditions, using *disabled* can be an important way to process their emotions and to self-identify.

Ultimately, it is essential to ask people about their preferred terminology, recognizing that language is not just a means of communication but a powerful tool in shaping self-identity and societal perception. As Pey Carter wrote to us,

It's not so different from how people in the LGBTQIA+ community choose their pronouns, or how people across cultures decide what language best reflects their identity. The words we use for ourselves matter—because they're ours.

For me, I say "disabled person." Not by accident, but by choice. Disability is not a footnote in my life; it's a defining part of who I am and the work I do. I am disabled. And too often, I've seen how easily that reality—mine and others'—is dismissed or softened into something more "palatable."

When I speak publicly, I use both "disabled people" and "people with disabilities." Not because I'm unsure, but because I want everyone to feel seen in the language that resonates with them.

What's striking though, is how often people—usually with good intentions—try to correct me. They suggest "person with disabilities," or worse, "differently abled," as if the word *disabled* is something shameful I should avoid. As if I need help reframing myself.

But those suggestions rarely come from a place of understanding my identity. More often, they come from a desire to make themselves more comfortable with it.

Language of pity. Phrases like "suffering from," "afflicted with," and "wheelchair-bound" make assumptions about how disabled people experience their disability and are associated with the medical and charity models of disability. To consider how this language influences perception, think of a person in a wheelchair. Quick: did you automatically picture them in a hospital or nursing home? Often disabled people are just living their lives, with all the ups and downs, challenges, and opportunities that life brings, and not suffering more than the average non-disabled person. Assuming that a disabled person is suffering as a result of their difference from the supposed "norm" detracts from the richness and diversity life offers and places the emphasis only on their supposed deviation from a standard. Even praise, however well intentioned, can perpetuate harmful stereotypes; rhapsodizing about how "wonderfully eloquent" a disabled person is, for instance, implicitly suggests that disabled people are not normally able to express themselves well.

Ableist idioms. The belief that disabilities are always problems rather than simply part of the diversity of the human condition, which is associated with the medical and charity models, leads to associating disabilities with failings and "normal" abilities with strength of character. Calling on people to, for instance, "stand up for justice" or "not take things sitting down" perpetuates these associations, even when nothing of the sort is intended. The ubiquitous idioms that use images of disability to convey criticism may seem harmless to non-disabled readers, but we ask you to trust that they land very differently with many people who have the conditions to which they allude. Saying that someone is "blind to the obvious," or calling them "lame" to mean "uncool," is derogatory toward people who are actually blind or have mobility impairments. (It is also derogatory to use outdated terminology, such as "lame," that harks back to an earlier era of judgment and misunderstanding.) When we say someone is "paralyzed with fear," we equate fear with a medical condition, negatively framing disability as something to be ashamed of and avoided. Describing someone as "crazy" because they've done something irrational trivializes mental health issues and perpetuates stigma, reducing complex human experience to an insult or label. These expressions may seem harmless in casual conversation, but they reflect and reinforce the devaluing and dismissal of disabled people.

Euphemisms. The word *disability* itself often carries a negative connotation for many, especially those using a medical or charity model, and they may try to soften its impact with euphemisms. Common euphemisms include phrases like "differently abled" or "special needs." The problem with these euphemisms is that they often disguise the truth, and the attempt to avoid the word *disability* can come across as condescending.[6] Euphemisms suggest that disability is to be shunned rather than acknowledged, which promotes two particularly harmful tendencies: expecting disabled people not to call attention to their disability by speaking up for themselves and isolating them to avoid causing non-disabled people discomfort or inconvenience.

Disability Justice

The disability justice movement, as distinct from the disability rights movement, calls us to recognize that the fight against ableism cannot be siloed, because ableism intersects with other forms of identity-based discrimination and marginalization. As we transition from disability rights to disability justice, we create space for crucial conversations about the intersectionality of identities. This approach was developed in 2005 by the

6 Amit Aggarwal, "The Dangers of Euphemisms in Disability Language," Accessibility Partners, May 8, 2024, accessibilitypartners.ca/the-dangers-of-euphemisms-in-disability-language/.

Disability Justice Collective, a group of queer disabled women of color: Patty Berne, Mia Mingus, and Stacey Milbern. It acknowledges that people's experiences are shaped by multiple aspects of their identities, such as race, gender, sexuality, age, and others, in addition to disability. For instance, a person may be Black, unhoused, queer, and disabled. Understanding and embracing intersectionality allows us to develop more comprehensive and inclusive strategies for promoting justice and equality.

The founders of the Disability Justice Collective were connected through an organization called Sins Invalid. They are a performance project centering disabled artists that carry on the disability justice framework that is "applied to the intersectional reexamination of a wide range of disability, human rights, and justice movements."[7]

---

7 Sins Invalid, sinsinvalid.org.

COMMON RESPONSES TO DISABLED PEOPLE

As disabled people move through the world, others often interact with them, and talk about disability in general, in ways that perpetuate harmful ideas and inhibit authentic engagement with them as whole people. It is useful to understand what these are so that you can recognize and resist them, both in others' behavior and in your own. Our intent here is not to provoke guilt. Rather, we hope you will recognize that you have absorbed ideas about disability from the culture around you. You have the opportunity now to reflect on the impact those ideas, and the behavior they promote, have on disabled people and to think and act differently in future.

It's often uncomfortable to confront our ignorance, but becoming aware of it is a critical first step. By asking thoughtful questions, approaching conversations with curiosity, and treating everyone with respect, we create space for open and authentic dialogue. Recognizing that disabled people lead complex and unique lives helps us move beyond stereotypes and assumptions. This shift allows congregations to reframe the narrative around disability, creating a culture of inclusion, understanding, and empowerment that values each person's lived experience.

Using Disabled People for Inspiration

Appropriating disabled people's accomplishments or survival to inspire non-disabled people reduces them to object lessons rather than individual people, valuable only in that they benefit the non-disabled. This appropriation is especially apparent in what the disability community calls "inspiration porn," which can take the form of, for instance, a news story about a developmentally delayed teen going to the prom or a poster showing an amputee doing something athletic with a motto like "What's your excuse?"

Liz Conejo: Media is filled with representations of disabled people as heroes and role models because they successfully do things that people without their disability can do. The problem here is that appropriating someone else's life experience for one's own use, without acknowledgment of that person's individuality or authentic connection with them, centers the interests of non-disabled people and ignores the disabled person's individuality and particular needs. Disabled people frequently point out that inspiration porn erases the necessity of adaptation, resourcefulness, and resilience just to live lives of autonomy and dignity by painting these traits as extraordinary.

A similar dynamic can show up in personal interactions, when a non-disabled person compliments a disabled person for simply living their life.

Dana Snyder-Grant: Are there things that people in the congregation do or say that are particularly unhelpful to my sense of belonging? Certainly. Now that the disability from MS is more visible, there have been a few incidents when parishioners have come up to me and offered comments that feel like microaggressions: "You are so brave" or "You have so much courage" or "You are my hero" are remarks that put me on a pedestal. They create a separation from me and a difference when I am othered like this. While I sense much love and respect, I also want to say, "Don't other me. I'm just like you. I happen to have a disability; this is just my life."

Kelly Riedesel: People ask me, "How are you?" and honestly, sometimes I'm feeling pretty lousy and I say so. Then they say, "If I felt like that, I couldn't do what you're doing. I'd be home in bed." If I stopped living and doing things I love every time I feel bad, I would have no life at all, which would make things worse. So I do things even when I feel bad, if they are important enough to me. It doesn't mean I'm not struggling, only that the struggle isn't getting the best of me (yet, anyway). I learned this skill in cognitive behavioral therapy, which I feel lucky to have access to consistently. This is a hard lesson to swallow, but it's important.

In critiquing inspiration porn, we in no way want to imply that it's wrong to learn from disabled people.

Imari S. Nuyen-Kariotis: We have unique perspectives and experiences that can enrich the lives of others. We can also be role models for other disabled people and people without disabilities. We can show them that it is possible to live a full and meaningful spiritual life with a disability.

The key word here is *unique*. Each disabled person has lived a life of particular experiences and lessons, and much can be learned from them in relationship and by paying attention to what they choose to share. Inspiration porn relies on othering disabled people and reducing their complex lives to a single, one-dimensional meaning.

Expecting Disabled People to Be Teachers

It is important to note that it should not be the job of disabled people to teach others how to treat them or to offer life lessons based on their disability. Disabled people are not living, breathing teachable moments. It is our hope that one day it won't be necessary for disabled people to share their personal stories and feelings in order to be treated with kindness and respect.

None of this is to say that disabled people don't want to share their perspectives and stories. Offering explicit and sincere invitations to disabled people to share their perspectives and stories is a gesture of welcome, respect, and connection. But sharing must be the disabled person's choice, not the non-disabled person's expectation.

Pity

Pity is another common response to disabled people. Non-disabled people may believe that all disabled people lead unhappy lives. Compassion and empathy are valuable, and they prompt non-disabled people to make sincere efforts to attend to disabled people's stories and to learn from them what supports they most want; these are expressions of Unitarian Universalist values. But pity creates an "us and them" division, often leading non-disabled people to conceive of disabled people as helpless and needy, and of themselves as therefore superior.

Lisa Ferris: Once a very nice woman from church helped me out when I was in a bind by babysitting my children for an afternoon. A few days later, I was at a church for a religious education meeting and I saw her in a Pastoral Care Committee meeting. I stopped in and said hi to the women there and thanked her again for babysitting for me. I told her that my kids enjoyed their time with her and that my son had drawn her a picture and I would bring it in for her on Sunday. Another woman in the group said, "Aw, that's what happens when they get too attached." They all laughed and went on to talk about how they have to be careful when they help "those people" and set boundaries so "they" don't have unrealistic expectations and depend on pastoral care too much. I froze. The wind seemed to leave my lungs as I listened to them talk about me and my family, along with others who might have received pastoral care, in the third person right in front of me. I had not known I was a "project" for them. I thought my family and I had just made a new friend and some day we would of course return the favor back to her like friends do. I felt like I would never really be seen as a fellow congregant who had gifts to contribute. It felt like my only role for them was to be needy so they could feel like they had done good deeds. I felt very much "othered," and I vowed that I would never seek help from the church for anything any more.

Pity also leads non-disabled people to consider disability inherently tragic. But disabled people beg to differ. Recall that the social model of disability points out that often people are disabled not by their limited functionality itself, but by societal attitudes and lack of appropriate support. Pity is aligned with the charity model, which fails to recognize the fullness and uniqueness of each person's identity, perspective, and life story.

Liz Conejo: My blindness has never been an issue for me; to the contrary, many members of our dysfunctional society prefer, and continue, to wear their own blinders, and this is the root cause of the many imposed barriers for those of us living with some kind of disability.

Conflation and Overgeneralization

Sometimes when people encounter a disabled person, they make erroneous assumptions based on that person's appearance or behavior. It's particularly common to conflate physical, cognitive, and mental health disabilities, such as by talking loudly and slowly to a blind person or treating someone who has trouble speaking like a child. Popular media and inaccurate or carelessly disseminated medical information can also lead people to overgeneralize about disability and erase a person's uniqueness.

Rev. Katie Norris: Assumptions about my neurodivergence in the faith communities I have belonged to were the result of the culture we live in. Despite ministers and congregants trying their hardest to be more welcoming, they only knew how to be welcoming based on false and exaggerated information they got from the media and the medical field.

Even people with the same disability experience it differently. Assuming that you know all about someone's disability because you've met someone else with the same one—or at least, one they use the same name for—puts an unfair burden on the disabled person to correct you. Overgeneralization is particularly insulting and patronizing when it leads to doubting someone's self-identification, disbelieving their accounts of their own experience, or presuming to teach them about their own disability. As Maria Zuccarello put it, "The community of people with disabilities is as diverse and dispersed as any other. We all have different needs, worldviews, and ways of interacting with the communities we live in."

Gale Callaghan: Folks want to learn about me, so very often I'll get questions like "Are you sure you're Autistic? You don't act anything like my cousin/nephew/grandchild." The spectrum nature of Autism means that no, I'm not necessarily going to act the same way that another person with the same disability does. I'm also not going to behave the way a child would.

Fear and Discomfort

Unfortunately, non-disabled people are often afraid of disability and try to avoid having to deal with it. The result is that disabled people are often shunned in both obvious and subtle ways. Under the medical and charity models, disabled people represent suffering and a stigmatized condition that should not be acknowledged, which can make non-disabled people feel that they don't know how to talk to or act around a disabled person. In trying to find something to say, they may resort to comparing them to other people with the same category of disability or predicting their future by analogy to others. This runs the risk of trivializing the person, avoiding engaging with them as their unique self. It can even be traumatizing to them.

Diana C. Archibald: What I remember most vividly about the coffee hour after I told my congregation I had Parkinson's is that a lot of people approached me. Some didn't say a word and just gave me a hug. Then there were the people who told me stories about their "Uncle Arnold who died from Parkinson's at seventy-eight." Or some horrific story of someone who had suffered so much in the end, and how "very sorry" they were for me. Not helpful. As we say in the Parkinson's community, "Everyone's Parkinson's is different."

It is better to be present and curious with a disabled person, which may lead to an honest exchange in which you acknowledge each other's humanity.

Sometimes members of a community worry that disabled people will ask too much of them. Disability can also trigger existential fears about what may be in all of our futures. As a result of these anxieties, the disabled person is isolated, perhaps treated politely or included in a superficial way but then ignored.

Lisa Ferris: In each church service, we were told that if we wanted to be members, we should talk to a board member to take the next steps. Over the years, I asked to become a member on at least four occasions, but no board member ever followed through with me to tell me what I needed to do.

Removing Disabled People from Public Awareness

Non-disabled people often assume that disabled people don't want to call attention to themselves. This assumption is usually well intentioned, and may in some cases even be true, but it can also be a convenient, if not wholly conscious, excuse for non-disabled people who are more comfortable when disability is non-apparent, and it can result in literally removing people from view and thereby isolating and even shaming them.

Anonymous: When I first started attending my UU church, I would pull my wheelchair up to the far end of the aisle. One day the minister showed me how he had removed chairs and created spaces for wheelchairs, scooters, and walkers. I was thrilled! I could sit closer to the action, where I could see better, and I got in the habit of coming in a little early to services so I could get situated in what I now called "my spot."

I had been proudly sitting there for a few weeks when I felt someone gently tap my shoulder and whisper in my ear. He said that I stuck up so high from others in the row that it was really noticeable to people watching online. He said he wanted to tell me "for my sake, as my friend." I've never sat there since.

I think of this often as I wasn't in anyone's way or blocking the view of the camera. It was brought to my attention as someone looking out for me, and yet it's something I'm ashamed of and causes me emotional grief.

Pey Carter: Sometimes the things that are particularly unhelpful or difficult for my sense of belonging are small, and sometimes they are big. One significant encounter was during an evening RE program I led. A person in attendance shared that they wished that when they were out in public, disabled people could just be in a corner so she wouldn't have to look at them because disabled people make her uncomfortable. Keep in mind, she knew I was disabled. This was extremely shocking and hurtful. I get, on some level, where this comes from. Many of us were taught as kids not to stare, not to notice, not to acknowledge people we perceived as disabled. That lesson, even if it was meant to be polite, quietly teaches us that disability is something uncomfortable—something to look away from. Something "less than."

Imari S. Nuyen-Kariotis: My daughter Caurel has autism, epilepsy, and cerebral palsy, and she is nonverbal. She is also very bright and understands what people are saying. She and I always stayed in the foyer during the service in case she got upset or was loud. There was a sound system so we could participate by listening. One Sunday, Caurel was having a hard time; she knelt on the floor and went into a fetal position and started rocking back and forth, making a murmuring sound.

A woman came into the foyer, looked disparagingly at Caurel, and said, "What is she doing here?" She turned up her nose and glared at me.

I took a breath. "Caurel is my daughter and a valuable member of our congregation. She's just as capable as anyone else, and she's a great help. You should be a bit more kind, as she knows where all the cookies are kept."

The woman looked at Caurel and frowned. "I don't know," she said. "It just seems strange."

"There's nothing strange about it," I said. "Caurel is a wonderful person, and she deserves to be treated with respect. Just because she has disabilities and you don't understand them doesn't mean you can't learn from her."

The woman sighed. "I guess you're right," she said. "I'm sorry for being rude."

"That's okay," I said. "We all make mistakes."

The woman smiled and turned to Caurel. "Hello," she said. "My name is Sarah."

Caurel looked up, smiled back, and waved, giggling a bit.

In time, Sarah learned that Caurel was an artist, and she was impressed by her work. They became friends and they often worked together at the coffee hour. They were a great team and always had a lot of fun.

One day, Sarah came up to me and said, "I'm so glad I met your family. Your family, especially Caurel, has taught me so much."

Caurel and Sarah's friendship is a reminder that everyone has something to offer. We should never judge someone based on their disabilities. We should always be open to learning about others and accepting them for who they are.

Helen Armstrong: Can we engage directly to learn how disabled people embody diverse experience? Ours is a faith that often centers leadership of those who are white, non-disabled, and have class privilege. Let's ask people with other lived experiences to share the stage and embrace the unknown. We need to let go of our need for control and risk the discomfort.

Intrusive Questions

Non-disabled people often ask disabled people about their disabilities. Sometimes the questions are motivated by a fear of disability and sometimes by a sincere desire to understand and be helpful. But no matter why they are asked, they can be intrusive, even prying. Such questioning often ignores the disabled person's dignity and right to privacy, as though they have an obligation to satisfy others' curiosity at their own expense, and can be frustrating, enraging, and exhausting. Questioners, no matter how well intentioned, need to remember that disabled people, like all people, deserve to decide for themselves what, when, with whom, and how much they want to share.

It's also important to understand that asking people to describe or relive a disabling event, a medical intervention, the symptoms or development of their disability, or the like can be traumatizing for them.

L. A. Wright: When I was young and people were told that my blood could not form a clot, it often triggered a fear response. Over and over, other children and many adults would ask, "Does that mean you will bleed to death if you cut yourself?"

I tried to brush away the anguished questions, but they sometimes kept me awake at night or crept into my dreams.

Asking about a disabled person's well-being may seem only kind, not intrusive. Certainly we encourage the expression of care and concern for disabled people, but it matters how often this question is asked, and how. Constantly being asked "How are you?" can become exhausting, especially if it's asked in a pitying tone, or by someone who isn't a close enough friend to be answered honestly on bad days, and most especially if it isn't accompanied by actual attempts to help. An inquiry that may be only a social reflex becomes something that the disabled person has to actively manage over and over again, deciding every time how much to mask and how much to share and trying to anticipate how their answer may be received. The question tends to focus the interaction, even the whole relationship, primarily on the person's disability rather than on their whole self.

Intrusive questions can be hardest on those people who are newly disabled or newly diagnosed and still learning about their conditions and needs.

Diana C. Archibald: The hardest thing was dealing with the well-meaning people in my church community who repeatedly, for months after I told them of my Parkinson's diagnosis, would say, "How *are* you?" Drawing out the *are* into a very long word was no doubt meant to emphasize it without having to name the disease. I suppose this is polite in a way, but I didn't want to be reminded of my disease every time I went to church. How am I? Well, I was fine until you brought up my PD? Or sometimes: I'm not doing well, but now is not the time for me to talk about it. I want to go get a snack and a cup of tea. Mostly, I just didn't want to hear the pity and the worry. "I'm fine," I would say. I wasn't.

I wish people would help take care of me, even just a little bit, at least by looking out for my safety. I wish my church would reach out to me, not to say in passing, "How are you?" I wish individual people who used to know me and care about me would say, "Can I come over and bring you a meal, and we can sit outside and visit and catch up? We miss you at First Parish."

We do not mean to suggest that it's necessary to treat a disabled person as if their disability does not exist. It's an important part of their lives and shouldn't be treated as a no-fly zone, but neither should it be the only thing you talk to them about. Mutuality, sincere interest in the whole person, mindfulness about time and place, and respect for privacy are key, the same as they are for respectful and considerate conversation with anyone.

Kevin Wilson: Several months into my attendance at church, I had settled into a routine—arrive at church before service, sit in the back pew, take in the sights and smells of the sanctuary. Then one member of the congregation sat down next to me and said, "Do you mind if I ask you a question?" "Here it comes," I thought to myself. "The one question everyone asks me, the one question that always determines how a friendship will go from here on." The question finally arrived: "I notice you walk with a limp. Is everything okay?" I answered the question the way I have a thousand times: "I'm okay. I have a disability called cerebral palsy that affects the way I walk."

I braced myself for the worst. In my experience, people had two reactions to hearing I had a disability. They either pitied me or were scared of me and stopped the conversation altogether. That didn't happen this time. This time there was no visible reaction. The person just thanked me for answering their question and the conversation continued. In fact, the question became a launching point for this person to tell me a part of their life story. I remember they looked scared as they asked a question of their own: "Do you know I'm gay?" I said no. They asked another question: "Does it bother you now that you know I am?" I said no, it didn't bother me. I could see the visible relief on their face, as if a big burden had been lifted off of their shoulders.

I have often wondered what prompted this individual to share that part of their story with me. Up until that point, we had only seen each other a few times, sharing the back pew, but we had never talked. The only explanation I can come up with is that they saw a kindred spirit, someone like themselves who had spent a lot of time hiding a part of themselves from the world around them. This simple exchange of questions and answers had a big impact on my journey. After that Sunday morning exchange, I knew I had found a safe place, my new church home.

Later in this book (page 71), we will discuss the importance of involving disabled people in accessibility and inclusion planning by asking what they need. These kinds of questions are not intrusive, especially if they lead to beneficial action. But asking people to justify their needs and preferences or go into more detail than they readily offer can be experienced as prying and even distrusting that their needs are legitimate. It's always a good practice to follow the disabled person's lead in how detailed and intimate the conversation becomes.

Fixing

Many of us have a natural desire to be helpful and solve problems. This can sometimes result in offering unsolicited and unwanted advice. Disabled people, especially those who have been navigating the world with their disability for years or even since birth, typically understand their own needs and how to address them. Offering advice without being asked can unintentionally reinforce the harmful notion that a person's disability is a problem to be solved or something inherently negative. It can even imply that the person's disability is their own fault because they have not tried hard enough or done the right things to cure it. Disabled people often encounter the same advice repeatedly, even though they may already be addressing whatever the issue is in their own way. Instead of assuming you know what might help (and they don't), it's far more valuable to listen and learn from their lived experiences. Doing this not only helps you avoid giving unnecessary advice but also enables you to begin to understand their perspectives—perspectives rooted in real, personal expertise. Allyship does not mean trying to "fix" or change disabled people, but instead celebrating the richness of their diversity, intersectionalities, and authentic lived experiences.

Helen Armstrong: I encourage all Unitarian Universalists to embrace disabled people with intersecting identities in our spaces. Listen to us with open curiosity and resist the urge to comment, offer advice, or center yourself in your response.

Rev. Katie Norris: Normalizing neurodiversity means that we move away from this idea that people who are neurodivergent need to be managed to get them to fit back into "normal" behavior and functioning. There is no normal. There are societal and cultural norms, which are all a construct. This idea that people need to fit back into normal not only does not allow us to show up as our full selves, but our community misses out on many amazing and beautiful things we can learn from the diversity of our brains.

Pey Carter: After service, a man came up to me with all these solutions on how I could find a job. I could work remotely, he said, and I'd be able to take my MDiv to absolutely any company and they would want to hire me on the spot. I tried to explain about doctor appointments, chronic fatigue, and pain, and he kept interrupting and interrupting. I saw a woman come up on my left with two children, looking excited to talk to me. As I turned to talk to them, the same man got in between and switched to giving me all the ways that I could prevent people from approaching me when I park. Eventually, I had to stop him in a firm manner I had never had to use before, to tell him that this was a perfect example of ableism because he thought he knew more about my body and situation than I did. He was telling me that I needed to be fixed, that I needed to make changes, when in reality it is others and society that need to change. His response was, "Well I was just trying to throw things at you to see if something would stick," to which I replied, "I'm not your dartboard."

It turned out that the mom and her two kids were excited to speak to me because they all had Ehlers-Danlos and had never met someone with it. I looked at them and told them that I hoped this was a good example on how to advocate for themselves.

People often try to fix me after service through a recommendation of a diet or a book or an alternative therapy. On some level, they mean well, but it can be harmful, especially if someone with a disability is struggling emotionally with their diagnosis.

Shelly Rohe: I had gone from being a right-hand-dominant want-to-be artist to a left-hand-dominant, rather clumsy person; from being a five-mile-a-day runner to a wheelchair user. I wasn't new to disability, having worked in the field most of my life, but I didn't know how to be. I didn't know how to act. I didn't want anyone telling me how I should live or that I was doing it "wrong." I was scared, I was angry, and I was frustrated. I suffered from ableism, both internalized and toward disability in general. Being around people at church who would accept me just as I was seemed like an impossibility. I was used to people looking at me with sympathy in their eyes and saying things that perpetuated the idea that I needed to be "fixed." Often I agreed and thought that if I could "get better" or "overcome my disability," I would be okay. I've learned so much since I was first diagnosed with cerebral cavernous angioma and gaining my subsequent disabilities; I no longer feel this way.

Assuming we know more about a person's disability than what they have shared with us silences and disempowers the disabled person, centers the non-disabled person, and impedes inclusion. What matters is empathetic curiosity and willingness to learn that center the experiences and needs of the individual person in their wholeness. Getting to know a disabled person means neither ignoring the disability nor proving how well you understand it, but creating a relationship of trust based on authentic engagement. In the context of that relationship, disabled people can be welcomed as their entire selves, including but not limited to their disability.

Judgment

Disabled people frequently find that non-disabled people are judging their self-sufficiency, their effort, their credibility, and their willingness to sacrifice for others' convenience. Practicing nonjudgment is one of the most powerful ways to support and uplift disabled people. Disabilities are often deeply connected with a person's socioeconomic status and life experiences, such as unemployment, homelessness, or struggles with addiction, especially if the disabled person also holds another marginalized identity as well. These intersections reveal the complexity of individual people's lives and highlight the need for understanding rather than assuming. By setting aside biases and genuinely listening to other people's stories, we can cultivate empathy, challenge our misconceptions, and create meaningful connections. This practice not only enriches our relationships but also contributes to building a more inclusive and compassionate congregation.

Disabled people are particularly vulnerable to the judgment of others when community members avoid getting to know them, so that they don't get the benefit of the doubt that people are more likely to extend to their friends and colleagues.

Lisa Ferris: Dwight and I were and still are friends and parenting partners. We never had a romantic or marriage-type relationship. We are a family unit, albeit untraditional. Dwight, who uses a wheelchair, went to the UU church largely because of me and, although he tried to stay engaged for several years, he eventually tired of the exclusion. Because of that and health issues, he no longer wanted to put forth the energy to go. Around the same time, I came to marry my husband Nik and we had a child together. Nik is totally blind and has some facial deformity. When Nik started going to church with me, the tone seemed to change for many people. It felt like we were even more excluded. At first, I thought it might be that it looked like I divorced Dwight and quickly married Nik and it was just odd for people that he was no longer around. But he was around in *my* life, and so I tried to explain that to people in the nicest way possible. I did not toss him out for another man! We are still coparenting together! It's good, no worries!

But then another church member had a very public and contentious divorce. And I saw how people supported both her and her ex-husband. It did not seem like people were too judgmental about divorce here. So what was wrong? People barely said "hi" to us. They hardly engaged us at all anymore. It wasn't everyone, but the climate had changed. Nik is as outgoing and friendly as they come, so what gives? I slowly came to the conclusion that it was because of how we now looked. Whereas they saw Dwight as a basically good-looking guy in a chair, Nik was capital-D Disabled. There was no denying it. He looked different, he moved differently, and because he was blind and couldn't help me visually, all of my low-vision quirks were now in full view. I had caught the disability cooties from Nik, and we made people much more uncomfortable than they had been when I was there with Dwight.

L. A. Wright: "What did you do to get that bruise?" or "Why are you limping today?" people would ask. If I explained that I had done nothing out of the ordinary to cause the injury, the questioner's face would show disbelief. It would be decades before I learned that these questions I was asked over and over again were microaggressions, leaving scars that would last much longer than the purple and blue marks on my skin. My memories of the physical pain disappeared like clouds in the sky, but the emotional memories hardened like stones. At that time, I tried to shrug off the questions and forget their skeptical reactions to my answers, but my anger quickened.

Kate Ryan: Unitarian Universalists have long embraced the American idea that people should be able to pull themselves up by their own bootstraps, that we should all be independent and should not need help, which goes directly at odds with the idea of disability justice, where interconnectedness and mutual aid are a guiding light for people who often, but not always, need more help or consideration than someone who is not disabled.

Did it ever occur to anyone that a church could run perfectly well if there were no people to mess things up? Because people mess up. Disabled people mess up. We are human beings and we have needs that can be hard to meet. One Sunday, I felt the urge to investigate a new chalice we had and accidentally spilled lamp oil everywhere. Lamp oil is not the easiest thing to clean up, but it could be cleaned up, just as all messes can be.

Even the symptoms and manifestations of disability itself are often interpreted as bad behavior, such as slurred speech being mistaken for drunkenness, inability to make eye contact being mistaken for evasiveness, inability to volunteer for certain kinds of work being mistaken for selfishness, and different ways of processing information being mistaken for inattentiveness. This kind of judgment tells people they are only lovable if they are not themselves.

Rev. Katie Norris: I have found that communities that constantly judge behavior they do not deem "normal" as disruptive are communities that lack trust. For example, I consulted with a congregation when they insisted a congregant who had trouble walking and slurred and jumbled speech was disruptive. They believed this person was consistently drunk at church and thus a danger to themselves and others. However, as a minister, I had information the congregation did not, which was that this person had a neurodegenerative disease, but I could not disclose health information. This person did not feel comfortable disclosing because what typically happens as soon as a neurodegenerative diagnosis is revealed is that people ostracize you. The congregation lacked trust in the person, the person lacked trust in the congregation, and the congregation judged behavior based on their own assumptions.

Sheri Thomas: If I was in a church small group meeting and I needed to stand up after sitting for a while, was that disruptive behavior? If I knit during church, is that disruptive? If I am in a meeting and get a panic attack and need to leave suddenly, is that disruptive? What exactly was disruptive behavior? According to most behavioral covenants, truly disruptive behavior would be not being in right relationship with another person.

Rev. Michelle LaGrave: When I was approaching the end of an interim ministry, a person came up to me at the end of a worship service. She said to me something along these lines—that she had a confession to make, that she had judged me superficially at first, that she was wrong to do so, that she was grateful for my ministry, and I would never fully know how deeply my ministry affected her. I didn't ask her how she judged me; I didn't feel like I had anything to forgive. What I do know is this: We are Unitarian Universalists and redemption is always possible.

Centering the Disability Instead of the Person

Often, when interacting with a disabled person, non-disabled people focus on the disability more than the person, reducing them to that one part of their identity. We've all done it. It's a cultural norm that shows up in the media we consume, what we are taught, and what is modeled for us by people in our lives. Sometimes even good intentions and anxiety about whether or not to explicitly acknowledge the disability can lead us to fixate on it.

While many claim *disabled* proudly as an identity, it's also true that people who have an apparent disability are often overidentified with their disabilities rather than perceived as whole people.

Lisa Ferris: One time, a person I had been acquainted with for years came up to me and started telling me about another blind mom who used to come to church with her husband who used a wheelchair. It took me a second to realize that he was talking about me and didn't realize I was the same person without Dwight with me. This slammed home for me that some people just really never saw past the disability at all.

L. A. Wright: If I had no visible bruises, I would hear how cute I was, or how smart. On other days, the injuries were all that most people saw when they looked at me. The other parts of me became invisible. Labeled as disabled, I was treated as an oddity, or troublesome. I also became a victim rather than a child, someone to pity or one who needed more help than most other children. I was treated differently. As I grew older, that difference was cruel punishment. I did not want to be seen as fragile, or out of sight. I wanted to be seen as the whole me.

Centering a Service Animal

One way that people often focus on the disability instead of the person is by paying attention to, or even trying to interact with, a service animal while ignoring its human handler.

Here are some guidelines for when you encounter a person with a service dog:

- Ask the handler. Before interacting with a service dog in any way, get the handler's permission. and ask how to best support them so that the service dog can do its job.
- Respect the dog's space. Don't block its movement or vision.
- Speak directly to the handler, not the dog.
- Don't touch, talk to, feed, or otherwise distract the dog.
- Don't give the dog commands. Only their handler should do this.
- Don't assume a napping dog is off-duty. A napping service dog is still at work.
- Don't approach a service dog with your own pet.
- Don't try to help the dog without their handler's permission.

Similar guidelines apply to other service animals.

Shelly Rohe: I have been out with a friend and their service animal and noticed how often people approached the person to talk about their dog. At first, I thought it was nice that people felt at ease talking with them. But then I noticed that it was never to engage my friend; rather it was to tell a story about their own pet. When I asked my friend about this, they confirmed that it was deflating to feel that they hadn't been acknowledged. They were just there to hear about the other person's personal story. I began to see this type of interaction as a missed opportunity.

Rev. Michelle LaGrave: At one conference I attended, I encountered a colleague while navigating a very long and steep stairway. My service dog Bella was with me. She was trained to go up and down stairs slowly and one stair at a time with the verbal command "easy." This is what we were doing when a colleague saw us and began to talk, almost gush, about how well Bella was doing on the stairs. As she shared her amazement over Bella on the stairs, I felt like I was not being seen for who I am. She never noticed that it was I who was challenged by the stairs, nor that Bella was going slowly for me. This colleague was later assigned, along with me, to a peer group that has been meeting monthly for years. I eventually talked with her about what happened on the stairs, and she is now one of my most trusted colleagues. I have certainly forgiven her, and I know, without a doubt, that she will always be there for me.

There is nothing like the feeling of being known and appreciated by a community for who you really are, of being able to simply be yourself. It is essential to spiritual well-being and something disabled people often struggle to find. It is also essential to the mission of UU congregations and the spiritual well-being of our communities.

Charlie Farrell: My wife Carol wanted to be recognized when she arrived at church with a big smile. Even though she may not have known other people's names, she knew who everyone was. She wanted to enter the building with as much dignity as possible, and we supported her with walking, and then with her wheelchair. She wanted to sit in a place where she could see and be seen, not placed in the back.

She wanted to understand the meaning of the service with a large-print summary of the message and to be able to socialize at coffee hour in a smaller group where people came up to talk to her. Carol did not want to be special or singled out. She said, "I just want to be me."

A subtle and insidious way of isolating disabled people is by assuming that their primary concerns, values, life issues, and interests are always connected to their disability. In fact, disabled people have the same sorts of concerns and interests that anyone else has, in addition to those caused or intensified by their disability. Non-disabled people who are anxious or performative about inclusion sometimes forget this and only engage with disabled people about their accessibility needs or assume that everything they say is really about their disability. Behaving as though the disabled person has nothing to say or offer on other subjects makes it difficult for them to build relationships with other community members.

One way to avoid this is to remember that everyone's concerns, values, and priorities are informed by their lived experiences. It's just that, for some people, disability is one of those experiences.

Rev. Tandi Rogers: My kryptonite is multitasking, forgetting to eat, shame, rushing, and insistence that I should "just try harder." But, truth be told, isn't that everyone's kryptonite? When the Unitarian Universalist communities began dismantling white supremacy culture, it was good for everyone. It certainly is liberating for me as a developmentally disabled person.

Dana Snyder-Grant: Living with illness is about being susceptible to loss and hurt. We all have vulnerabilities. Your friends may have more money than you do, you divorce, you lose your job, a loved one dies. We are susceptible to loss, all the time, to the losses that come from being human. The community of care in Unitarian Universalism recognizes and accepts that joy and sorrow sit within us at one and the same time. Living with disability is its mirror.

Trivialization

Some congregational leaders don't consider disability inclusion to be a priority, so problems are simply not addressed. Disabled people who ask for adaptations to help them be included are too often treated as if they are being unreasonable and making a big deal out of nothing, denying the truth of their lived experience.

Pey Carter: Conversations about language can seem small, but those shifts matter. Simple changes—like saying "rise in body or spirit" or "side with love"—help more people feel included.

It's easy to dismiss this as being overly literal or too sensitive, but that overlooks the daily microaggressions people experience, even in welcoming spaces. Words shape belonging, and when people pause to listen and say, "I never thought about that," it can make all the difference. This is when I feel like I belong, like I am home.

Gale Callaghan: Sometimes I'll share an experience and receive a response like "Everyone's a little Autistic. I feel just the same way sometimes." Reactions like this, though well-meaning, are ultimately harmful. This says to me, "I don't see you. I don't understand your experience, and I'm not willing to."

Resentment and Silencing

Disabled people are often treated as if they are imposing a burden on non-disabled people by asking for changes to be made so they can participate. Sometimes disabled people are even treated as troublemakers because of their requests.

Kate Ryan: The more involved I got in the disability justice community, the more I stood up for my own rights and refused to accommodate myself but expected my church to provide these things, the more dissatisfied I became in the church and the less tolerant they became of me. I will never forget when a good friend on the nominating committee told me that I would never be asked to serve on a committee because people did not like me and I caused discord.

April Smith: The assumption that disabled individuals are burdensome or require special treatment is an attitudinal barrier, and a pervasive belief in our society as a whole. This attitudinal barrier can lead to disabled congregants feeling resentment and exclusion as if they are set apart from the rest of the congregation.

Distrust

Having to ask for help or accommodation in one's community is inherently a vulnerable position. Sadly, that vulnerability is often met with distrust, an unwillingness to believe that the person's needs are real. Sometimes disabled people are told that they don't understand their own lived experience correctly or that their perceptions are unreliable because of their disability.

Rev. Katie Norris: Many of my stories I can't share publicly. Since some of my neurodivergence includes that I have mental illness, it can be pretty complex because I am still not sure that those of us with mental health differences can show up as our full selves. It is unsafe for us to talk about some of the experiences we have had in our churches because of the stigma against mental illness. Often we are told that our lived experience is wrong, or that we interpreted events incorrectly because of our mental illness. Over the past nineteen years, I have seen the climate improve in many churches. I feel that we are just now turning the corner of understanding how to be truly welcoming, to hear from people with lived experience, believe them, and give them what they need.

Defensiveness

In some cases, congregational leaders are defensive and argumentative when the subject of accommodations for and inclusion of disabled people is brought up. They may react as though the people raising these topics are making accusations rather than expressing faith that they are sincerely committed to living the congregation's values and interested in learning how to do that better.

April Smith: When I pointed out that what they said was ableist and why, this person backtracked and tried to change the meaning of what they said. They were more concerned with getting their point across and having everyone agree with them than having an actual conversation about why what they said was inappropriate. There's a term for this: it's called gaslighting, and it has no place in our congregation.

While this member and I eventually came to a sort of understanding of each other, I still don't fully believe that the inherent ableism that was displayed and how it affects others were fully understood by this person.

Lisa Ferris: The first time I ever went to a Unitarian Universalist church, the door was locked.

I am blind and hearing impaired, and at that time, I was pregnant with twins. My parenting partner, Dwight, has quadriplegia and uses a wheelchair. We were excited to get up on Sunday morning and have this new experience. We were new to the neighborhood and really wanted to find a positive and supportive community in which to raise our children. I had researched Unitarian Universalism online, and it looked like exactly what we wanted: a church community low on dogma, open to diverse families, and high on doing good deeds to make the world a better place.

We had noticed a long, triple-level ramp that had been built on the backside of the building as we had walked by in previous weeks, and we took it as a good sign that disabled people were welcome there.

But when we arrived and climbed the long ramp on that first Sunday, the door wouldn't open. We knocked but got no response. After waiting a few minutes, I told Dwight to wait there. Grabbing the underside of my protruding pregnant belly, the only slightly comfortable way to walk anymore, I went back down the three levels of decline, worked my way around the church and up the flight of stairs at the front of the building. I was welcomed when I entered the door, but not knowing the building myself, I had to ask several people to help me get to the back door where my partner waited so I could let him in.

We were not too fazed. Maybe someone just forgot today or didn't grab it yet. No problem. It barely raised a concern for us, and we enjoyed the service. Afterward, a few people came up to us and politely welcomed us. So far, so good. But then it was locked the next week too. And a few times after that. It was locked approximately half the time we went. When we finally brought it up to the minister, we just thought it was a procedural problem. We knew there were probably a number of rotating volunteers who got the church ready on Sunday morning. I thought it just needed to be added to a checklist and the problem would be solved. I was shocked at the response we got.

The interim minister was very defensive. He told us that the door was not being kept locked to keep us out on purpose but it got stuck a lot. This didn't quite make sense to me because I was often the one who went around and physically unlocked the latched door, but I do suppose it was possible. We told the minister that we did not think the intent was to keep us out but the effect was the same. We couldn't get into the building. I had newborn twins at this time, and between the wheelchair, the twins in car seats and their stroller, and my poor vision, it was quite a difficult task to get into the church. And it also meant that Dwight or anyone else who needed ramp access could not get in on their own. We asked that a solution be found, not that blame be sought. The problem got marginally better over the next few years, but never completely got solved. Even when we did get in that entrance, there was no one there to greet us or give us an order of service like at the other entrance. In an old church, we understood the difficulties of architectural accessibility. We did not expect perfection. But it would have been nice to feel welcomed on Sunday mornings instead of worrying what rigamarole we might be faced with to even get in.

One thing that attracted me to the Unitarian Universalists was this notion that everyone is choosing to be here, everyone has come together to do good, to be a good person, to feel good and help others feel good. That is very powerful and can be a huge motivation for change. But only if the need to be seen as good doesn't become a barrier to actually doing good works.

Once I wrote about my confusion about the UU church in a blog post titled "I Think I Am an Alien." Somehow it got to the minister. I was just about to have my twins dedicated in a UU church service when he wrote to me asking how I could want to have my kids dedicated if I hated the church so much. But I never hated the church. I felt like the church hated me and people like me and I didn't know how to change it. I broke down and cried. I was so confused. When I tried to make things work for me, I was met with such defensiveness and derision that I wasn't grateful enough for the little things someone might have already done for me.

It's natural to feel bad when we are told that we have harmed someone. We all want to feel that we are good people, and even constructive feedback can trigger feelings of shame or anger. And yet over and over again in the stories that disabled people sent us, we see evidence that combating ableism in ourselves and in our practices is a complex process that is never finished. There is no one comprehensive checklist of accommodations that can ensure perfect inclusion for everyone. There is no guarantee that we can welcome and include everyone, no matter how hard we try. But that is not an excuse for not trying. Each person who finds a place to belong and grow and give and receive love and spiritual nourishment because the community is intentional about inclusion matters. The goal is to keep making room for more, not to reach perfection.

It is important to be willing to step outside of your comfort zone and embrace moments of discomfort. Recognize that mistakes will happen, and true transformation occurs when we learn and grow from them.

Rev. Katie Norris: Were any of the assumptions people made about me and what it means to be neurodivergent intentionally malicious? No. In fact, at least they talked about it and I was allowed in the community. Most people in other communities just made assumptions and shut me out.

We are a covenantal faith, and that means that we promise to treat each other with dignity and respect, and when we fall short of that covenant, we revisit that promise, revise it if necessary, and try again.

Here is what I love about our faith (well, one of the many things I love): We are always learning and doing better. The road is often bumpy and not pleasant all the time, but most people are willing to hear from people actually living with neurodivergence, those of us with lived experience. They are willing to change systems so that they become more welcoming.

April Smith: When I first started thinking about what I wanted to say for this book, I was approaching this whole situation with a lot of anger, and honestly, a lot of bias. I didn't understand why disability justice and accessibility were such hard concepts for people to grasp, and I didn't understand the unwillingness of people to do whatever they could to make things more accessible.

Through some uncomfortable conversations, and by working closely with an ally, I learned that there can be a really huge learning curve for those who aren't disabled. And that I'm biased to see everything through the lens of disability because it's something that's always been in my life—whether it was family members or my own disabilities that I was learning to live with.

This doesn't mean the lack of accessibility and accommodations in my congregation is justified, or that the resistance by others is excusable.

Lisa Ferris: My disability is a bit hard for people to understand. I have some vision and some hearing. Sometimes it might have seemed like I had no problems at all hearing or seeing what was going on; other times I was unable to use my vision and hearing effectively without alternatives and accommodations. I have always understood that no one, not even my closest friends and family, can truly understand when I can or can't see or hear something. They would regularly misinterpret when I needed accommodation or what kind. This has always been understandable to me, and I have never expected perfection. I never expect everyone I meet to be experts in ADA accessibility or in how blind, deaf, or otherwise disabled people do everything. What I and most other disabled people like me hope for is to be included. We want to be welcomed and seen as contributing members just like anybody else. If something isn't working, if we can't access something, we want people around us to be willing to work it out with us until it works. To be adaptable to change and to prioritize inclusion.

Lisa Holcomb: Unitarian Universalism historically, empathically, and emphatically embodies the phrase "When we know better, we do better." For me and other disabled and chronically ill people both like and unlike me, that makes all the difference. We know we are seen and heard and cared for.

Gale Callaghan: I've experienced micro, and macro, aggressions every day of my life. UUs are the first group of people I've met who learn from being called out and always work on growing. It is impossible to know what you've never learned, and Unitarian Universalists are always working to learn.

ACCESSIBILITY AND INCLUSION

As we turn to accessibility and inclusion, let's admit up front that no congregation will ever be able to truthfully declare that it has made itself fully accessible to every single person who wants to join the community. Every new person, whether disabled or not, who enters the congregation brings with them their own unique set of needs. Different people's needs may conflict with each other. And the needs of existing members change over time. In addition, no one can educate themselves on everything about every disability. But none of this is an excuse for not striving to be as inclusive, welcoming, and affirming of disabled people as you can be. Our Unitarian Universalist values, with love at the center of all we do, are hollow if they are not lived out in our communities. In this section, we will offer some general ways to think about accessibility and inclusion to help you with this work.

Use Universal Design

The term "universal design" was coined by the architect Ronald Mace, who defined it as "the design of products and environments to be usable by all people, to the greatest extent possible, without the need for adaptation or specialized design."[8] When members of your community resist changes aimed at

8 Center for Universal Design, North Carolina State University, 1997, design.ncsu.edu/research/center-for-universal-design.

better including disabled people, it can be helpful to teach them about universal design and explain that it doesn't mean taking extraordinary measures for the benefit of a few; rather, it benefits the whole community. For instance, clear, large print signage benefits people with limited vision but also helps people unfamiliar with a space navigate it more easily. Similarly, features like automatic doors or adjustable-height desks serve disabled people while offering convenience to everyone. Universal design moves away from requiring people to request accommodations, instead focusing on enhancing functionality and usability for everyone. This perspective promotes equity and the goal of a society where all people can participate fully and comfortably in everyday activities.

Julia Fitzer: Efforts to improve accessibility for people with hearing loss also promote the inclusion of children, older adults, people who speak English as a second language, and people with auditory processing disorders. The brain pathways responsible for processing sound, especially in noisy conditions, do not fully develop until the teen years. Older adults may have increased trouble with background noise as the brain changes with age.

Universal design principles can be beneficially applied not just to the physical infrastructure of the congregation's buildings and other spaces but also to operations and communications, leading to offerings such as multiplatform meetings, documents in large print and digital formats, and a variety of content appropriate for different learning styles.

Rev. Jennifer DeBusk Alviar: I have attended many Unitarian Universalist worship services and social justice retreats that provided value-rich content. However, I often left feeling exhausted. Why? Because the verbal content was not paired with visual, kinesthetic, and experiential learning grounded in the natural world. Too much stimulation, not enough soul.

I wondered: Was I the only one who experienced this kind of exhaustion? Might there be others who could benefit from a slower pace? More quietude? A longing for greater embodiment? A deeper connection to ecology and soul?

Over many years of preaching as a guest minister to Unitarian Universalist congregations across the Pacific Northwest, I have developed a multisensory, somatic approach to designing and leading worship services. I wanted to model a more inclusive style of worship that met my own cognitive needs. This, along with fostering greater inclusion for others in broadening the scope of diverse learning styles.

Here are some of the valuable insights I discovered through my experiential process of adapting worship in congregational life to reflect a more holistic approach. When we design sacred spaces for congregants to engage their minds and bodies through sensory touch, movement, nature, art, and ritual as part of worship, it creates a space of safety and inclusion. This becomes a grace-filled space where all brains and bodies feel welcomed. A sacred space of worth, dignity, respect, and belonging. A thoughtfully designed space of inclusion that benefits everyone. This is the gift of universal design.

Often congregations resist making large-scale efforts at improving accessibility because of a deeply held but unexamined belief that such efforts will result in an environment that is depressing, sterile, boring, and laborious. Those of us who are experienced in accessibility work know the opposite to be true. When more people can access the environment without struggle, it becomes vibrant, thriving, humming with connection, and warmly inviting. We encourage you to enter into all your accessibility projects with a sense of joy and beauty.

Disabled People's Needs Aren't "Special"

Congregations often resist making mindful efforts to fully include disabled people because they have absorbed the wider culture's idea that needs related to disability are "special needs" and efforts to meet them are "special treatment." But the truth is that we all have special needs and all of us, whether disabled or not, need some form of accommodation. As Rev. Katie Norris pointed out to us, "Any change you make to your environment to make things accessible for you, like adjusting the seat in your car, is an accommodation."

Lisa Ferris: An issue that came up often in AIM's work was the issue of disability accommodations being seen as "extra" and "special," such that they were funded by much smaller discretionary "pastoral care" funding rather than incorporated into the operating budget. People with disabilities do not have "special needs." Their needs are the same as everyone else's. Everyone needs accommodations to be able to participate in church life.

When disability accommodations are framed as "pastoral care," it says a lot about what type of people are prioritized as being welcome in the church. If printed orders of service are an operating cost, why would Braille or digital orders of service not also be an operating cost? Both are accommodations. If parking lots are operating costs, why would there need to be a special fundraiser to make accessible parking spaces? If PA systems are an operating cost, why aren't assistive listening devices? Why are accommodations for non-disabled people expected but those for disabled folks are optional and "extra"? Many of them, when integrated from the ground up, don't even cost any more than typical accommodations. Budget restraints are difficult everywhere, but people with disabilities should not always be the group that is sacrificed, burdened, and excluded by them. Singling out one group for these types of burdens is the very definition of systemic oppression.

Looking to everyone's needs as a matter of course, rather than singling out disabled people, both helps the congregation to better serve all of its members and avoids stigmatizing disabled people as asking for something extra. For instance, committee leaders can make a practice of asking if everyone in a meeting is able to access the committee's documents and has enough time to process them. This is helpful not only to people who process information in a certain way due to disability but also to people with very busy schedules and technology challenges and makes it much easier for everyone to advocate for themselves.

Rev. Katie Norris: What does a congregation that is welcoming look like in everyday life? This is what it looked like for me recently, when I was given my first solo with the church choir. I do not easily remember a song, or even a line of a song. After I learn the song correctly, which takes a long time, I have to practice it dozens and dozens of time, exactly the same way every time, exactly as it will be performed with the other musicians. My brain does not work like many other people's, where they go over something three to five times and have it down. At first, my old fears kicked in, assuming that I could not ask for what I needed to be able to do this thing that I love and give back to the congregation that is so important to me. However, this church has trust and it has normalized accommodations. I had experienced membership being welcoming of all different kinds of physical and neurological needs of people in the church. This also showed me that people led with understanding first, and not judgment. So I did something I never would have done before. I asked for what I needed. I needed to record the music director playing the accompaniment to the song and I needed to record certain parts with him singing exactly what I was supposed to sing so I could practice it at home over and over again. No one batted an eye. No one said that if I could not get the song quickly I must not have been paying attention or that I was wasting people's time. It was literally a non-event.

I also feel very comfortable at this church saying that I am neurodivergent and letting people know when I might need some assistance with things around volunteering or guest preaching.

This might seem simple, but when you are neurodivergent, you have typically been told no, you can't have any accommodation, which means we often cannot participate in church or give back to the church. We are stuck, allowed to be ourselves, but not too much ourselves.

When we see people included in ways that work for them, in everyday church life, we know we are welcome, and that changes everything.

Learn What Your Community Needs

Checking in regularly about everyone's needs in the day-to-day operations and programs of your congregation helps to ensure accessibility in the moment, but making more long-term changes requires a more proactive approach. One of the challenges of accessibility work is the idea that universal accessibility is impossible, which can make people feel overwhelmed and inhibit their progress. So we recommend that you focus at first on meeting the needs of the people in your community. But don't think only about the ones you already know about! As we've discussed, there are many non-apparent disabilities, and even if you know about someone's disabilities, you don't know what accommodations would most benefit them if you have not asked them. And some people may feel more comfortable being honest about their needs anonymously. So a good concrete first action is a congregational survey.

When sending out a survey, it is important to consider how responses to it, including requests for accommodations, will be handled. Even if you believe you know every member of the congregation as well as you know your own family, survey responses may surprise you. They may drive home the importance of things your congregation already knows it needs to work on; they may also bring to light problems that have never been addressed or perhaps even publicly acknowledged. Agree in advance which committees will be responsible for addressing what kinds of requests. If you have a dedicated accessibility team, be sure each member's area of responsibility is clear. Links to sample surveys can be found on page 206. After you have assessed the congregation's needs and prioritized the projects you will work on, the real action can begin.

A congregation should not focus on "checking off the boxes" for accessibility; instead, be honest and transparent about how your congregation is accessible and what needs work. We have found that simply drawing attention to a need creates an opportunity for change.

Don't Ignore Competing Needs

We won't pretend that accessibility isn't complex. Sometimes changes are made to better meet the needs of one group of disabled people, but those changes disadvantage another group. Often there is no perfect solution for everyone, but mindfulness and dialogue can help maximize accessibility and minimize harm for as many people as possible. Of course disabled people should be involved in decision making, but it's still always worth asking whether some other disabled people are being left out. It can hurt when a congregation congratulates itself on improving accessibility (for some) through actions that also reduce accessibility (for others).

Julia Fitzer: It hurt when my UU friends from other congregations proudly posted UUA memes on Facebook and boasted how virtuous they were for requiring masks and protecting the most vulnerable. These memes and posts ignored the needs of a group of people who were especially vulnerable to social and employment challenges during the pandemic shut-downs: deaf and hard of hearing people.

If the memes and posts from my UU friends had also reminded folks to reach out to deaf and hard of hearing members of congregations in outdoor spaces or over Zoom, the messages would have felt much more inclusive. It would not have hurt.

My local congregation was faced with balancing the needs of different groups of members with board policy on vaccinations, masking, and social distancing. The board had a tough, thankless job. I don't know if I could have come up with better policies. I just wanted my UU friends to quit saying that masks were harmless pieces of cloth, as if the visual aspect of communication did not matter.

Involve Disabled People in Planning

Although churches and other places of worship in the US are not legally obligated to meet ADA requirements, many will naturally turn to the ADA guidelines pertaining to public buildings (available at ada.gov). These can be a good place to start, since most people are at least aware that they exist, but they are far from comprehensive and not sufficient in themselves. They describe only minimum standards for accessibility and inclusivity. Places of worship, which are more spiritually and emotionally significant than most public buildings, should aspire to do better.

The truth is that no checklist or set of regulations can replace relationships and listening as the foundations for accessibility and inclusion. No authority outside of the community can tell you about the needs of the people within it. You must have strong and trusting relationships with the disabled members of your congregation, so that they feel safe telling you what they need, and you must listen to what they tell you rather than treating them like a problem to be solved. The latter too often leads to "accommodations" that are incomplete and don't actually improve access. Remember that accessibility needs are very individual, and may differ even among people who share the same name for their disability. Instead of presuming you know what actions to take, what language to use, or whether assistance is needed, communicate directly and respectfully with the disabled members of your community. Disabled people are the best judges of their own needs and preferences. Accessibility plans that are made without their participation may result in unfulfilled promises of inclusion or empty performative gestures.

Rev. Diane Teichert: I showed up for one preaching gig where they had told me there were handrails on the right for going up and going down the chancel, but it turned out they were so artistic that they were useless. Yes, they look great, but that wasn't very welcoming. They had a ramp, so I was able to do the service. I just had to use my scooter to get up there instead of walking. I would have preferred to climb the stairs.

Not only will consulting with disabled people result in better accessibility solutions, it will also give them an opportunity to take leadership roles in an area where they are experts, drawing them further into leadership in the congregation and fostering a greater sense of belonging. Making it easy for them to share what they know with you communicates that you take the work of inclusion seriously and value their participation and presence in your shared community.

It is essential to involve disabled people from the very beginning of the process, following the motto "Nothing about us without us," which the disability rights community often shortens to "Nothing without us." This principle is not limited to individual projects but should also extend to all aspects of congregational life.

Kaden Colton: I became involved with the Antiracism Committee meetings at the congregation. This committee was relatively small. One of the people I met through this committee was Harold Straughan. A question he asked me after one of the meetings was "What do you need to thrive?" This question deeply resonated with me. I did not expect to have such a thought-provoking and caring question posed to me.

Anonymous: From initial research to installation and testing I was left out of the process. This was both hurtful and inefficient. As the only knowledgeable person with hearing loss, it would have been helpful for me to be part of each step to learn enough to serve as a back-up resource about the nature of the systems and installation issues as well as why decisions were made as they were. I could also point out issues that might not be caught during testing by people with normal hearing.

I was eventually able to establish myself as the congregation's Hearing Loss Volunteer by identifying which committee chair to approach and providing them with a list of the things that needed to be done, and my commitment to doing them.

Maintain Equity and Independence

Not consulting disabled people in accessibility planning often results in accommodations that meet people's needs only partially or not at all, or are demeaning or isolating to disabled people. This happens because the planners focus on solving the "problem" rather than on the experience of the disabled people using the accommodation. For many congregations, involving disabled people in making decisions about accommodations requires an attitudinal shift.

Congregations must remember that the goal is not simply access but equitable access, in which everyone can participate equally easily without having to ask for help. Many disabled people want to blend into their community's life as seamlessly as possible, doing things the same way, or nearly the same way, that everyone else does. For example, disabled people would like to enter a building without being carried or attend a committee meeting with others rather than being told they will just have to read the minutes because the meeting is in an inaccessible house.

Lisa Holcomb: As a person with physical disabilities that come and go, one thing I love about my UU congregation is that if I needed to come in a wheelchair, I could roll straight from my car down into the building with no issues. Other churches in our area claim to be 100-percent accessible but have these weird areas where you cannot get from one parking spot to another or one floor to another without going out of your way, wasting your time and effort. They put the onus of this extra time and energy use on the already disadvantaged person rather than doing construction to make things more equitable. Not so in this Unitarian Universalist building. I can get anywhere by wheels or crutches or braced foot. Unless you've lived the experience of having to go around, you don't understand just how wonderful it is to just follow the same path others are going down.

April Smith: While I've been fortunate to have people around me to help hold doors open when needed, I know this would be a barrier to my access if I were alone. Additionally, relying on others as a disabled person is something that should always be an option, not a necessity. Personally, I prefer to be as self-sufficient as possible to maintain my own sense of empowerment and agency over my body and experience.

Shelly Rohe: I use a power wheelchair that weighs almost four hundred pounds without me in it. When accessibility information is not on the website of the establishment that I will visit, I call ahead to inquire about accessibility. I have been told on numerous occasions that they can get me in by carrying me and lifting my wheelchair up the steps. This would be impossible for anyone! A building is not accessible if anyone else needs to be there to help me gain access. It's not acceptable for a person to have to sacrifice autonomy and rely on the presence of others.

April Smith: In addition to meetings on Zoom that didn't have captions available, I've also had the experience of a very important series of congregational meetings scheduled with no Zoom option at all! This was extremely strange to me, as we've had multiple congregational meetings that were hybrid to include those who were only able to attend virtually. While there were options offered as Zoom only, they were not the same as the ones scheduled only as in person, taking away my ability to participate in congregational life and business in a way that was equitable.

Anonymous: I was asked to be part of a chalice circle and was extremely excited about it. I went to every meeting and participated every chance I had. I learned a lot and felt my comfort level with the group grow with every meeting. At the end of each year, they chose to have a group dinner at a restaurant in town. I use a wheelchair and the restaurant was up a flight of steps. They had no way in for me except through the loading dock and kitchen. I was mortified. The group told me they were more than happy to carry me up the steps and bring my wheelchair to me. I asked if there were other choices of restaurants. The group voted to stick with their original choice. I was shocked. I felt like I had been on an even playing field with everyone else and now I was "different" or "other." I was not about to be carried up a flight of stairs; nor was I willing to go in the back entrance through the kitchen. I will work with this establishment on following ADA regulations. As for the chalice circle, I didn't attend the dinner. Nor have I ever gone back.

Often the "accommodations" that are offered without consulting disabled people are themselves isolating, sequestering disabled people in out-of-the-way spaces.

Rev. Katie Norris: We do want to be mindful that the accommodations we use are the ones we have asked people who are neurodivergent if they even want, and that the accommodations do not fall into this idea that separating us out means the church is being accessible. In fact, one way that people often assume they are being welcoming to people with dementia, or any neurotype that makes it difficult to sit still in worship or meetings, is to make space for them—meaning sending them to a different area of the church, which is actually not welcoming. In one church, they had pews in the back reserved for people who like to knit or write or otherwise not sit perfectly still during worship. This was also where the wheelchair seating was. This is an old form of accommodations that we have been taught—to create a separate space for people, which really just sends us away from our community, not only isolating us, but also not giving the community access to our gifts and contributions. There will always be people for whom a quiet space, or a space that is louder and with more movement, is helpful, or an affinity small group ministry may be desired. However, I have found that the first thing many people do is send us away, to our space, to be with other people like us, rather than integrating us into the larger community.

Value Adaptive Participation

One way that disabled people are often treated inequitably is relatively subtle and indirect, but very impactful. When disabled people take advantage of adaptations to participate in the life of the congregation, that adaptive mode of participation is sometimes not valued equally with participation in the more traditional ways.

April Smith: One attitudinal barrier that I frequently and continuously seem to struggle against is the belief that physical presence and interactions are more valuable than online attendance and participation. In my previous congregation, a member said that in order to draw in a new minister, we need to become a "congregation of presence" after talking about how there isn't a lot of physical attendance in our congregation these days.

Take Collective Responsibility

While it is essential to ask people about their specific accessibility needs to ensure their full inclusion in congregational life, it is equally important not to solely rely on this approach. Making disabled people solely responsible for their own inclusion only reinforces the feeling, among disabled and non-disabled members alike, that they are not truly part of the community and reinforces the oppressive nature of ableism. Therefore, a comprehensive approach that involves the entire congregation is necessary to foster true accessibility and inclusivity. Common patterns that place an unfair burden on disabled people include

- asking them to educate the entire congregation with a prepared presentation instead of giving them the opportunity to share their expertise in a way that is more comfortable for them
- asking them to justify their needs
- asking them to speak about the needs of other disabled people

- asking them to come up with solutions that don't inconvenience others
- springing personal or challenging questions on them in inappropriate settings

The emotional impact of being asked to educate others is complicated. It's affected by the person's history and personality, their emotional state that day, the context in which questions are asked, the expectations that other people have of the person, and other factors. Congregations shouldn't expect that disabled people all feel the same way about their disability or disability in general (or about any other topic, for that matter), or even that the same person feels the same way about it all the time. So it's good practice to keep questions invitational rather than probing and general rather than specific, and follow the disabled person's lead in the conversation.

Anonymous: As one of the few people in my congregation who is open about my disability, I find it exhausting to be asked about how our congregation can be more accessible. Why is it my responsibility? I find myself fielding questions that I have no idea about just because I am the token disabled person. I might not even have a certain kind of disability, say hearing, and yet I'm asked about hearing loops and sign language interpreters. I can generally tell people where to look for answers, but then when it comes to questions about my own disability, sometimes I get frustrated and don't know what to say.

Dana Snyder-Grant: With the support of an ally, whether professional or lay, I've had some honest conversations with others. In the world of increased awareness of the ways in which dominant culture interacts with those on the margins, we are invited into these conversations. I'm used to wearing my pedagogic hat as a social worker and teacher and person with a disability. In fact, I may feel empowered by these roles and own these conversations, even while, at the same time, I may feel burdened by them. This is yet another spiritual teaching that has been reinforced for me from Unitarian Universalism: we are both/and.

April Smith: As a disabled person (whose identity also intersects many other marginalized communities), I've struggled with being forced to accept "good enough" accommodations for my needs in ways that are not equivalent to what is offered to those with different abilities and needs. When I've tried to bring these experiences of microaggression and ableism to the attention of those making these decisions, instead of being able to engage in meaningful conversation about how to do better as a whole, I've gotten pushback and defensiveness, as well as being asked to do the emotional labor of educating others on what ableism and microaggressions are.

Audre Lorde once said, "Whenever the need for some pretense of communication arises, those who profit from our oppression call upon us to share our knowledge with them. In other words, it is the responsibility of the oppressed to teach the oppressors their mistakes. . . . Women are expected to educate men. Lesbians and gay men are expected to educate the heterosexual world. The oppressors maintain their position and evade responsibility for their own actions."

And in my experience, this goes for disabled people as well.

But I realize now that no one can be expected to come to an understanding of concepts like disability justice and accessibility on their own. Sometimes they need someone who's been through it to help educate and guide them. And while I had initially taken the stance of "it's not my job to educate people," I now feel like it kind of is, actually—if for no other reason than to show them why learning and researching about disability justice on their own is an important pursuit.

While I still believe that in the digital age, there is ample opportunity for people to do their own research and find solutions to defining and overcoming their own ableism, I also understand that some people need more motivation to be able to begin this work. I also believe that it's the responsibility of the congregations to come together as allies and work to dismantle the ableist ideals they are helping to uphold. And if that means stepping up to help educate my congregation to work toward this goal, then I now gladly accept this role.

Maria Zuccarello: This important work requires both disabled and non-disabled congregants to ask questions, not make assumptions. It requires steps to be taken together, not alone. It requires a look into all aspects of church life and participation. It requires all of us to interweave our individual experiences into a shared existence that we are all responsible for. Once we share the responsibility of joining our lived experiences into an interdependent worldview, we can own our own ideal of working for a better world within the congregation and work side by side to bring that work to the community at large.

Rev. Katie Norris: It is helpful if people who are neurotypical do some education on their own, as it is a lot of extra work to put onto people who are neurodivergent, to ask us to educate others all the time. However, it is also necessary to actually ask people who are neurodivergent what we want and need. And we need to be included and at the forefront of the changes that are made.

It's important to be mindful as well of the fact that many disabled people have a long history of sharing their needs only to have them ignored, dismissed, judged, or met with promises that are never fulfilled. When you ask disabled people to share their needs and experiences with you, you have an obligation to follow up with timely action that is informed by what you have learned.

The congregation's collective responsibility for accessibility includes training its members in how accommodations are to be made available and used. Often physical accommodations are put in place but the human element is neglected, so that the accommodations actually reinforce the barriers they are intended to dismantle.

Julia Fitzer: Only a portion of the deaf and hard of hearing community knows sign language. Most people lose hearing acuity as they age and some seek hearing aids. Some UU congregations offer ASL interpreters. I do not know of any that offer live captioning by trained stenographers, which would meet the needs of a greater range of people. Many UU congregations offer assisted listening devices. In my experience, these systems are often poorly maintained, and volunteer ushers are unfamiliar with their basic operations.

Neva Allen: When my husband and I moved and started attending a new church, we noticed some things right away that caused us trouble in accessing it. The first was the entryway. At the front of the building were stairs, and at the side was a ramp that I could use in my power chair. However, there were times that the door on the side was locked. I spoke to the minister about how I didn't feel that was okay, and she assured me that it didn't happen often but did happen more than it should have.

As a new member of the church, I decided to join the Social Action Committee. I asked the committee to help me make the town more accessible to people with mobility challenges. With the help of my husband, the church community, the town council, and the businesses, the one-year campaign to make the town more accessible was a success. We started with our town being only 20 percent accessible, and by the end, it was 80 percent accessible.

After this very successful campaign, I decided to go to a sale at the church. I was so distressed when I found the side door locked again. Not only that, but a sales rack had been in front of it on the inside, so that when someone who happened by said to someone that I was outside, it took them several minutes to remove the rack and unlock the door.

I almost left the church that day. I was so distraught. Of course, nobody had thought about people who have mobility challenges when they had planned the sale. It felt like all the work we had done was a waste. My minister came and talked to me and told how very sorry they were, and so I decided to stay.

April Smith: When my previous congregation made each in-person meeting hybrid, there were still problems with them not being interactive enough; oftentimes there was no one monitoring the chat, and in one meeting, the host of the physical group admitted to "forgetting there were online participants." So while some progress was made in adding more accessible options, there's definitely some work to be done.

Treating accessibility as a collective responsibility means not leaving it up to just a few people in the congregation to take the initiative and follow through. The congregation as a whole needs to be invested in accessibility and committed to working for and upholding it. Not only will this result in better decisions and faster, more effective accommodations, but it will make improving accessibility a much less daunting prospect and lessen resistance to it, especially the common excuse that it would be too inconvenient or difficult. As we've said, accessibility work can get complex. Sometimes it involves difficult decisions and uncertainty. It often requires humility, and it often must be done against some people's wishes. No one should have to carry this responsibility alone.

Rev. Katie Norris: If more resources were needed, it was not assumed that the leader of the group could create them. Maybe that was not in their wheelhouse, but for someone else in the group, it was an easy task for them to do.

Leadership Must Lead

While congregations have collective responsibility for creating an inclusive environment in which all can participate equally and feel welcomed and valued as they are, congregational leaders have a special obligation to create this shared sense of commitment. Leadership needs to set expectations about how requests for accommodation will be handled and to make clear that everyone in a leadership position—staff, committee members, religious education personnel, and others—has a responsibility to respond to such requests, either themselves or in collaboration with other appropriate leaders. Nor should they have to make up a response on the spot. To ensure full inclusion and address ableism effectively, it is essential to clearly define in your policies how the needs of disabled people will be met and how ableism will be explicitly addressed. Doing this, and clearly, consistently, and transparently communicating these responsibilities and policies to the whole community, demonstrates a commitment to creating a welcoming and inclusive space for all members.

Lisa Ferris: There are a lot of nice, good people in the UU church. As I write, I imagine that some people reading know me and might be thinking, "I had no idea anything like this happened in my church." And here is where we find the crux of the problem.

When I think back on my ten years of UU experiences at multiple congregations and levels of leadership and try to find the running theme through what I and many others with disabilities experienced, the common thread seems to be leadership failures. People didn't know about my issues because they were never told; nor did they see any action taken by leadership to mitigate them. Time and time again, on all levels, both disabled and non-disabled congregants tried to improve things in big and small ways, but when they went to leadership, it fell through. I can only theorize about why this might be the case.

The only thing I can come up with is this story I remember from early on in my UU experience. We had a service where the minister answered anonymous questions that people had submitted to a box the week before. He picked out a question and read it to himself and sighed. The congregation laughed. I wondered what difficult question this could be. It turned out that it was my question. I had asked why there were not more racial minorities and disabled folks in the congregation or Unitarian Universalism at large and what could be done to be more inclusive. He paused for a minute and then answered. "This is up to you," he said. "There is nothing leaders can do about it without you all. It has to come from you." And he shoved the question away and picked another one.

In a democratic organization of associations like the UUA, individuals do have a lot of responsibility for what happens within. And it does take everyone to do the work of change and to make an organization more inclusive for all types of people. But leadership has to lead. In all of my work within UU organizations, I always had individual supporters. People wished us well. But often, it stopped with leadership. They were often "too busy" for people with disabilities, and the budget was "too tight" to touch. Leaders are put in these positions to see the big picture, help set priorities, and organize and direct action. It is hard to reach the correct balance of being directed by constituents and overdirecting them. It isn't always going to be perfect. But when a concerted effort is needed to effect change, leaders need to set the standard.

It has been several years since I effectively ended my participation in Unitarian Universalism. I hope that perhaps changes for the better have been made in those years. But I was disheartened to find out that the AIM Project, for which I had such high hopes, has ended its certification program after only eight congregations became certified after a decade of work. I still feel that there are a lot of well-meaning people who want congregational life that is more welcoming and inclusive of people with disabilities, but they have not been able to effectively organize for more immediate action because they do not appear to have much support from their leaders.

Change the Rules

At the heart of disability inclusion is a commitment to prioritizing the manifestation of our community values. Inclusion should be more important to us than the way we've always done things, comfort with the status quo, and strict adherence to rules that don't fit us all equally. It means changing how we do things to fit our people instead of trying to change our people to fit how we do things.

Rev. Katie Norris: Having strict rules about how everything needs to be done and then consequences for not following every rule is terrifying, and it shows that I cannot trust this group because if I do anything outside their norms, I will be in trouble. And I definitely can't ask for accommodations because we have to follow the rules!

Penny Clipperton: When I applied for congregational membership for both myself and my son, Ian, who is not able to speak or write, I was told that I would be welcome as a member but that the bylaws require that new members sign the membership book and participate verbally in a ceremony. Ian would only be able to join as an associate. I said that would be like being a "memberette," like a Ladies Auxiliary member of the Legion. And what about the first three Principles of Unitarian Universalism at that time? The inherent worth and dignity of every person; justice, equity, and compassion in human relations; and acceptance of one another and encouragement to spiritual growth in our congregations? I spoke to Rev. Debra about not joining until Ian could become a full member, but she suggested that as a member, I would have more influence over making changes to the bylaws. And so I became a member and Debra took this situation to the Membership Committee.

Barbara Lane: When we received Ian's application for membership, we had a meeting to discuss how to proceed. We agreed that Ian's behavior indicated that he feels a part of our community and that we wanted to be inclusive and act with compassion. We realized that the requirements for membership excluded not only Ian, but anyone who cannot read, write, or speak.

The Membership Committee recommended to the Board a waiver of these requirements and that Ian be affirmed as a member of our church. Members of the Board stated it was their duty to uphold the bylaws and suggested the membership bylaws be revised before considering Ian's application for membership.

So Penny, Heather Walker, and I formed a subcommittee and got busy researching membership bylaws and inclusion in Unitarian Universalist communities. Between the three of us, we looked at a lot of material. The sources that I found the most helpful were the First Unitarian Congregation of Toronto bylaws, the section of the Unitarian Universalist Association website on membership bylaws, and my daughter, who was a law student at the time.

The Membership Committee worked hard to draft a bylaw amendment that would provide membership to someone who, like Ian, senses and responds to spiritual life within the congregation without being able to express his experience and commitment in words.

The bylaw revision was presented to the congregation at the May 2016 congregational meeting. There was some discussion, although not as much contentious as it was supportive. Hazel Corcoran, a member who also happens to be a lawyer, suggested a minor wording change, and the amended motion was passed. Bylaw 1.1.1 reads,

> In the event that a person sixteen years of age or older is unable to fulfill the requirements in 1.1 due to a difference in physical and/or mental abilities or other exceptional circumstances, the Board may grant membership to the person by majority vote.

After the vote, someone at the back of the room called out, "It's about time!" Later in the year, the Membership Committee resubmitted Ian's membership application to the Board and it was affirmed.

On November 18, 2018, at a special Sunday service designed expressly for the purpose, we welcomed Ian as a full member of Calgary Unitarians. He was very excited. He wore his kilt and was assisted to light the chalice.

The membership chair welcomed Ian with these words: "Your presence is a gift to us all. We thank you for becoming a part of this religious community that is searching for truth, struggling for justice, and attempting to live in love." The minister said, "Ian, you are so generous in bringing your whole self! Your joy in being here is evident, your presence so welcome. We know you love candles and the chalice, so here is one for your own home. May it remind you always of how loved you are."

Prioritize Need Over Convenience

A particularly harmful argument that is often raised against requests for accommodation is that the suggested action would be "inconvenient" or less than ideal for the majority of the congregation. Unitarian Universalism is a tradition that values democracy, and many may believe that this tyranny of the majority is justified. But the important comparison here is not between numbers of people who benefit on either side of the decision, but between wants and needs. Rejecting accommodations as inconvenient sends a message that the congregation values the wants of people who are not disabled over the needs of the disabled, and therefore that it values disabled people less than other members.

It can help to remind your community that disabled people are inconvenienced and forced to compromise all the time. They may have to bring their own food because they can't eat the food supplied, or sit in an anteroom because their wheelchair can't get into the main sanctuary, or arrange for a special RE teacher because their child needs extra care, or restrict their fluid intake before going to service because the building doesn't have an accessible bathroom, or bring their own microphone because the community doesn't provide one, or bear many other kinds of extra burdens. People without disabilities have the privilege of not having to worry about these situations. If non-disabled people were willing to give up some of this privilege in order to provide accommodations to disabled people, this would go a long way to making the congregation a place where the disabled people feel like they belong.

Lisa Ferris: I have a severe/profound hearing loss and use hearing aids. I tried to mitigate my problems hearing the sermons by sitting up front. But it seemed to cause problems with the flow in the aisles when Dwight's wheelchair blocked the aisle. There were spaces for wheelchairs in back, but then I would really just be sitting there, cut off from both the visual and audio aspects of the service. I found out that the sermon transcripts were available to read after the service. This gave me an idea. Could I possibly get the sermon sent to me beforehand in an email? Then I could read along with it by having my laptop speech reader read it to me. A very kind woman asked the minister if he could do this. He declined, saying there was no way he could remember in time and have it ready even five minutes before the service. These kinds of responses almost physically hurt, like punches to the stomach. They made me feel like I was asking for too much, like I didn't matter, and like I wasn't really wanted there. This response to disability is not rare, it is universal. So why would it be any different in this community?

Rev. Katie Norris: It's always so interesting to me that church kitchens have labels on all the cabinets and instructions printed out for the coffee maker, but when someone asks for printed instructions for something in a board meeting, people think it's weird or selfish by requiring more work from the group.

Lisa Ferris: Sometimes, several people would go to an indoor playground after the service together so their kids could play, but we could not get there without a car. I understand that not everyone has room in their car for extra people, but when I suggested a different indoor playground that I could easily get to by light rail, I was told they didn't like that one and they were sorry we just couldn't go. I didn't care so much, but it was hard on my children, who heard through the kids about the plans and knew they weren't going to be invited.

April Smith: I once attended a very important small group meeting via Zoom, where there wasn't an option for captions (though they've been made available for all other meetings I've attended with this congregation.) When I brought this up, it resulted in other attendees feeling frustrated that it was taking time away from the meeting, even though they showed up late! Additionally, they had no problem expressing their frustration, which really added a sour note to my experience. This is a fine example of ableism and microaggressions at work. Fortunately, everyone has been taught how to enable captions at Zoom meetings, and this has not continued to be a problem. But the reality is that it shouldn't have been a problem in the first place, and I certainly shouldn't have been shamed for requesting that my needs be met so I could fully participate in the meeting.

Lisa Ferris: Some of the congregations have real challenges to accessibility, like churches on the historical register that could not be easily architecturally modified. Budget was always an issue as well. But often the biggest challenge seemed to me to be that no one really cared, beyond the committee. Most of the tension was between the committee who wanted to implement the AIM program and the church staff and Board of Directors. Some challenges were just based on silliness. One church had a large lower and small upper parking lot. The larger lower parking lot had a long flight of outdoor cement steps to get to the church entrance. The smaller upper parking lot had no such barrier to entrance but was reserved for the minister and staff. It seemed easy enough to me to change at least some of the upper parking lot into disabled parking. But the ministry refused to do that because then the entire staff wouldn't fit there. They chose to close off their church to disabled and elderly people to keep their parking lot. Many times, it isn't that something can't be done; it is that it is just not that important to anyone.

On the whole, the Unitarian Universalists I met were not better or worse than the general population as far as how they chose to include disabled people. But because there are no ADA or other disability civil rights laws to fall back on when dealing with religious organizations, all efforts to make churches welcoming to disabled people are voluntary. Whenever I hear anyone say that no one is against the disabled and that people just don't know any better and are confused about the ADA, I think of the Unitarian Universalists. They could have voluntarily done a lot to include disabled folks. They had a lot of resources and help to learn how, and simply chose not to.

Don't Make People Ask

When disabled people arrive in a community, specific and transparent communications about accessibility can alleviate their anxiety about how to navigate the space and the awkwardness of having to ask, so that they can focus on whether the congregation can become their spiritual home rather than on logistics. EqUUal Access recommends that one of the first and most important things a congregation can do is to clearly document their accessibility on their website so that people can check this out before visiting. The situation need not—probably cannot—be perfect, but the website should honestly and thoroughly describe it. AIM developed a set of guidelines to help congregations understand what information they should offer on their websites, and these are available at equualaccess.org under the EA Resources tab.[9]

Rev. Diane Teichert: Post the little wheelchair symbol on your website but don't leave it at that. You should also list exactly what you've got because it is very discouraging and a little humiliating to have to call up and ask these questions. So why not say clearly on the website? And if you're holding an event outdoors, you need to say how easy it is going to be for people to hear and for people to get there physically. The more explicit invitations can be, the more welcoming they are to all kinds of people.

Kaden Colton: I could still read regular-sized print if I held the book up to the bridge of my nose. This made me feel awkward during services when everyone else was asked to open a hymnal to a specific song or read the order of service. I had difficulty as time progressed being able to read the words as I lost more sight. I didn't know large-print hymnals were available until I had been attending for a few years.

---

9 "Website Accessibility," EqUUal Access, equualaccess.org/resources-2/congregational-accessibility-projects/website-accessibility.

Being clear about what is and is not available allows disabled people to know what accommodations to request before visiting and, more importantly, what they will not even need to ask for. This is important because a person's spiritual exploration is very personal, and they may not want to involve anyone in their choice to attend services with your congregation. A clear description of accessibility is also helpful to everyone in your congregation who is involved in outreach and hospitality. Similarly, disabled people in your community, whether visiting or members, deserve to know what the process is for considering accommodation requests, especially if the accommodation cannot be made immediately.

Rev. Katie Norris: Part of normalizing accommodations is putting in options that no one has to ask for, like we do (hopefully in all of our churches) with curb ramps (wheelchair ramps) and handrails. Assisted listening devices, seats throughout the sanctuary that do not have armrests, wayfinding signs so people know where things are, making it a cultural norm to leave a bit of processing time in conversations so people can respond, large-print orders of service, words projected during the service, a few quiet sections if your coffee hour is in a big space with lots of people, and noting in meetings that it's okay to get up when you need to.

If we normalize different ways of being in the world, then we are all included. No one has to disclose a diagnosis of their neurotype if they do not want, or cannot (and truthfully, many people cannot).

Coming to a congregation and finding that they don't have to ask for accommodations, because they have already been made, can be emotionally powerful for a disabled person. It is a strong sign of welcome and a signal that this could be a place where they won't have to fight for acceptance.

Lisa Holcomb: As a neurodivergent person, I have trouble being in certain kinds of buildings. It's hard to know if I'll be somewhere I feel comfortable. I need windows to stare out of so I don't get claustrophobic, and this building has so many. The lights don't make flickering sounds. There aren't flashing lights or a huge vibrating organ to jangle my senses. It is a calm, well-thought-out building.

As a new member of the worship team, I now understand how much care is put into every aspect of the service, but even before I became enlightened to the behind-the-scenes details, I could feel the embrace of the thoughtfulness that inspired them. There are quiet moments for those who need time and space to either mentally or physically recover from singing or standing. There are wordings used to make sure that everyone feels welcomed and seen. As a writer, words are always of the utmost importance to me, but as a frequently physically distressed human being used to hearing "if you are able" regarding standing during the service, it is so soothing to hear "if you are comfortable doing so." I don't know why it makes a difference, but it does, and someone at the UU church thought of that and made that change. I love that.

Keep Reassessing

Each person follows a unique path toward understanding accessibility for both themselves and others. We also know that change is inevitable, and what works for most people right now may not work so well for anyone later on. People's needs change, the membership of your community changes, and technologies and understandings evolve. Page 206 has links to surveys that can be posted on your website so that people can fill it out repeatedly as their needs change. Or you might want to conduct a follow-up survey every one to two years. Frequently resurveying your community and reassessing its needs can lead you to make new or different decisions about which accessibility solutions will work for the greatest number of people. The work of inclusion is never finished but requires sustained commitment. Many voices are needed, and there are many opportunities ahead of us.

Address Social Barriers

Social isolation doesn't only happen when someone is unable to attend gatherings or when they are ignored once there. It can also happen because of a variety of other disability-related barriers to social interaction that may not be immediately obvious to others. Difficulty communicating in ways familiar to others, moving around the gathering space, standing or sitting for an extended period, managing food while standing, or hearing or understanding speech over music or other background noise can isolate people even in the midst of a gathering. Mindfully thinking through these factors while planning events can help congregations avoid excluding disabled people.

Food and drink play a central role in many social functions, fostering a sense of community and togetherness. Consider the diverse needs of people with autoimmune disabilities, food allergies, and disabilities that affect the ability to hold a plate or handle utensils, especially while standing. Providing diverse food options, clearly labeling ingredients, and promoting awareness of different needs around food and eating can help to ensure that all attendees can enjoy their meal comfortably and focus on connecting with others.

Ginny Vaughan: The biggest obstacle is buffet-style meals at the church. Even before I was using the walker, I could never participate independently in buffets. Luckily, my husband is always with me to make a plate for me. Because I have trouble with fine motor tasks, I am not a very neat eater. I am very self-conscious of the way I eat and do not like to eat with people I'm not familiar with. At my church, we have Souper Sundays once a month to fundraise for the religious education program. I am in a small minority of people who do not like soup because of the difficulty of eating it.

Social interaction with new people or in new situations is already difficult for a lot of people without any disability. For various reasons, it can be especially difficult or awkward for disabled people to say that they are uncomfortable or need something. And sometimes it isn't easy to know who to ask or what to ask for.

Ginny Vaughan: Because of my disability, coffee hour is not enjoyable for me. Although there are chairs to sit in, most people prefer to stand and talk. I am not always the most vocal at telling people what I need, like a chair. Also, because of the noise level at coffee hour, it is harder for people to understand my speech.

Charlie Farrell: Most people living with dementia have some degree of progressive memory loss and a diminished ability to speak. Often we are unable to tell you what we need and what we want. This happens to me. If you focus on trying to find the emotional connection and emotional needs, this gets rid of a lot of frustration and confusion.

We can still participate in groups, worship, and social time if we are given more time to respond in conversations, if people in groups do not talk over each other, and if you can ask us directly how we are feeling and what we need or want. If I struggle to find a word, ask me to tell you a story about what I am trying to say. I can see what I want to talk about, but often I can't find the exact words I need to say. Telling you a story about it helps. Using objects, like a picture or an item, for us to look at and talk about together can help. It is hard for us to just think of words and then say them.

Kelly Riedesel: After service at coffee hour, I may be in the middle of a conversation but desperately need to sit down. I don't want to stop the conversation to do so, but when I'm standing for very long, my weak blood vessels can't squeeze hard enough, so blood begins pooling in my legs and I start to feel really bad. It's hard to balance the desire to finish the conversation with the brain fog and feeling like I'm going to pass out.

When we notice someone struggling in a community we know to be caring, we may assume that someone else is helping them and we can move on. Sometimes that means that no one helps and the person is left to manage on their own, which can be a very lonely feeling. Getting to know someone helps you to understand their disability, know what accommodations might be helpful to them, and take simple, unintrusive steps to make things easier.

Julia Fitzer: I stood alone outside the nature center where the church was meeting, watching my fellow congregants gather into groups inside for post-service conversation. I waited some time, only a few short steps away on the adjacent patio area, before leaving in frustration. I was holding a lot inside of me, including loneliness, anxiety about shifting my career path and job searching, anger over political gaslighting after the January 6 attack on the Capitol, concern about climate change, supporting aging parents through serious health crises, loss of a significant relationship, depression, and navigating a masked pandemic world as a deaf person who relies on lipreading to supplement the input from a cochlear implant.

I had been part of this church for seven years now. Members appreciated my organization skills, loved my creative auction emails, and ate my vegan cooking experiments. They built my confidence when they asked me to serve a term as their president.

I was not intentionally left alone. The policy had just been changed to make masks optional outdoors, and many people there probably did not know that I had asked for the policy change so I that I could have some in-person human connection. I could have gone inside and grabbed people if I wanted, and people would have come outside.

Still, I had been president of the congregation when the pandemic hit in March of 2020 and devoted many hours to learning Zoom and making sure that people stayed connected with Zoom Bingo and Zoom Pictionary game nights. Thus it seemed ironic that after working so hard to maintain connections early in the pandemic, the effort was not being reciprocated.

Lisa Ferris: An example of how things aren't always perfect but can be made to work if people work together is our experience with the UU Family Camp. There was no way Dwight could go to family camp due to the inaccessibility of the sleeping arrangements and bathrooms, but my young twins and I went. Sometimes when a disabled person has never experienced something, it is impossible to know what you might need as far as accommodations. I had never attended anything like a church camp before. This was also the first year that the camp was put on by the church, so kinks were inevitable. On the first morning, I went down with my kids to eat breakfast in the dining hall and then went back to the room I was staying in for just a few minutes to drop off some things and let my newly potty-trained toddlers hit the restroom. When I came out, everyone was gone. I didn't know where they were, so I started walking around. Then my kids started happily playing in the sand volleyball court. So we just stayed there and played. I didn't really know what I was supposed to do. When lunch time came around, the people were back in the dining hall so we returned there, and I got so busy just trying to figure out what the food was and help my kids through the buffet line that no one really talked to me and I didn't get a chance to ask questions. Then in the afternoon, everyone was gone again. Poof! So we played on a nearby playground and just entertained ourselves. I was getting really distraught though. It was just exhausting to keep track of my toddlers and just figure out my own way around. And no one seemed to notice or care that we were struggling through the buffet line and all by ourselves all day. I ended up calling Dwight and asking him to come pick us up two days early. I made some excuse and left.

I felt like I failed but I didn't exactly know how or why or what to do to prevent it. It wasn't until a year later that I found out that there was a print agenda of activities with a map of where they would be that I was never given or told about. They were all off doing different camp and religious activities and I was left behind. I did not know there were going to be formal activities that people would all go to together. Sometimes you don't know what to ask! Sara Cloe came to my rescue and gave me the courage to try again. I told her what would be helpful to me. Could someone tell me what food was in the buffet line and perhaps help my kids and me get through it? Could someone just let me know what is on the itinerary and walk me to the next activities? Sara and her two teenage daughters completely came through for me that next year and the following year as well. The girls were always there the instant that I came into the dining hall to grab a plate for one of my kids and tell me what food was being served. I always knew what activities were going on and where they were. I was able to participate in many activities, and we all had a very good time. I was also able to help clean up when I was given the chance to be shown where to put things.

Offer Opportunities to Contribute

Perhaps the most damaging result of isolating disabled people, treating them primarily as problems to be solved, and judging them is that both they and their communities miss out on the very real gifts they have to offer. Disabled people don't want to merely participate or receive care from the congregation; just as much as anyone else, they want to offer something back to their communities and be valued for what they have to give. If that means inviting a disabled person to take a leadership role or give a presentation, it's well worth figuring out how to meet any logistical challenges and ensure they have the support they need to do so. Disabled people deserve the opportunity to be more than passive attendees, and your community deserves what they have to offer.

Imari S. Nuyen-Kariotis: I want to bring my whole self to my UU congregation. I want to be able to be myself, without having to hide or change who I am. I want to be able to worship and experience life in my congregation in the same way that everyone else does. I want to be able to contribute to my congregation and to make a difference in the world.

Kaden Colton: One of the memories I have of being involved at this congregation was when the minister asked the trans people she knew to put together and lead a service related to the Transgender Day of Remembrance. In 2019, I was one of three or four people to say yes on planning and leading this service. Each of us took different aspects of the service. I volunteered to cover the Time for All Ages and sing as a member of the choir.

I ended up picking the children's story *I Am Jazz*, by Jazz Jennings, for the Time for All Ages. I ended up creating a hard copy version of the story in Braille. I asked if the director of religious education would be able to hold up the picture book for the youth to see while I read. I also used Braille to have some notes for when I shared my story about finding Unitarian Universalism and finding South Valley Unitarian Universalist Society. I also worked with the staff of the congregation to obtain Braille copies of the information presented in a slideshow about the trans people and people perceived to be trans whose lives were cut short by violence.

The service went well. I quite enjoyed being able to help direct, participate, and ensure the service was more accessible to everyone who attended. It felt liberating being able to share a part of myself and being validated as a whole person in a religious/spiritual community. This experience in planning and leading a service got me excited about participating in future services outside of the choir, or participating more in the religious education classes.

Unfortunately society often reduces disabled people to a single label or uses their disability as an excuse to dismiss their capabilities, potential, or even humanity. Harmful stereotypes and double standards hold disabled people to expectations that are either unfairly high or dismissively low.

Rev. Amanda Schuber: I've found over the years that either I'm not seen as disabled enough to ask for accommodations or my disability is seen as limiting and requires me to be saved from any potential burden. This infuriating whiplash of identity has played out again and again over the years in congregations, my ministry, and other UU spaces. It's like being on a seesaw, dropping back and forth between extremes of identity that don't quite fit me.

Rev. Katie Norris: My community ministry is as a trauma-informed Montessori-based dementia care specialist. By far the most common thing people living with dementia tell me is that as soon as they say they have dementia, people start taking things away from them. Removing them from leadership and volunteer positions, telling them that they can sit in the "crying room" during church, and addressing their partner rather than talking directly to the person with dementia.

At the same time, the entire community needs to understand that when a disabled person, or really anyone, declines to contribute in a particular way, it does not mean they are less committed, less engaged, or less willing to help than anyone else, or that they don't have significant skills and capacities to offer. Disabled people are often giving their faith community everything they can, and that deserves appreciation, not comparison to what other community members do.

Diana C. Archibald: Regardless of the troubling nature of my symptoms, my baseline demeanor is optimistic and positive, and my drive to remain a productive member of society and change agent is very strong. I keep going and try to ignore my symptoms. My efforts have paid off, too. I continue to teach full-time, mentor students, and publish my research, and I also create art and garden. That is what people mostly see—a vibrant and accomplished woman who seems to be doing great. And I am. Except when I'm not.

Kate Ryan: As I get older and my body deteriorates due to my disabilities, I know that I am not as able to contribute to church in the ways that I used to. Sometimes I wish people understood that I am just as enthusiastic and excited as ever about everything, but my body and my brain demand that I slow down, that I do less.

Kelly Riedesel: I recently realized that I volunteer at church less than I'd really like to because I don't want to sign up to volunteer and then need to back out at the last minute, leaving nobody to do the task I volunteered for. I once volunteered to go to the Mountain Retreat and Learning Center to help with a youth program. My back went into a spasm the day before and I couldn't go, so somebody else had to step up at the last minute. I felt bad about that even though I couldn't help it. And so I don't volunteer much anymore. It occurs to me now that what I need is a volunteer buddy so if I can't fulfill my task, the buddy is prepared to step in.

Another barrier to my participation at church is that a lot of the meetings are in the evening. I'm often too tired and in too much pain by this part of the day. I understand the need for evening events because the evening is when everybody else can make it, because most people work. I don't see a lot that can be done as far as accessibility, inclusion, and accommodation in this situation, as it's hard to support for pain and fatigue.

In different situations, people will do things that are surprisingly relieving in their simplicity. The assistant director of faith development at our church leads the writing groups. She asked me to read one of the poems I wrote for the writing group out loud at our

Sunday service recently, helping me feel I can contribute deeply to the community with only my words.

People who know me well at church will ask me when I'm helping out if I need help with my helping. For example, I sometimes take the laundry from the church kitchen and bring it home to wash. When I'm taking it or returning it, whoever's there at church that day, if they know me, will say, "Hey, can I help you carry the baskets?" Again, I feel known and seen, and it's wonderful to be able to help without feeling diminished by the task.

The church's covenant encourages people to be helpers, to be good listeners, to be present and share their gifts. The people I have gotten to know at my congregation are the people who are sharing their gifts and presence with me, and that's what I need the most. When you have bodily limitations you can't change, money and time itself don't matter. So, as Mr. Rogers said, "Look for the helpers." And keep trying to find ways to be a helper. Lately for me, that's been reading my poetry out loud in various settings at church, which I never, ever would have done before. If you are struggling in life with disabilities, don't give up. In my mind, it doesn't really matter what your disability looks like; there are ways for everybody to receive and give. Keep trying different avenues. We often don't have the confidence to offer our help to others because we think it won't be enough. We underestimate the impact it can have. Trust yourself and what you have to give. There is a place for you.

What I wish my church community could understand is that I don't feel inside how I look outside. Just because I can do something one day doesn't mean I can do it the next day, or just because I'm smiling doesn't mean I'm not in pain or struggling with other symptoms. I'm a super responsible person in general. It's hard for me to say no when I'm asked to help with something. And because I don't necessarily look disabled on the outside, when I say no (a boundary I've had to learn) I don't know if people understand. I try not to take their responses personally. I always feel like I must have an elevator speech about why I'm saying no today when I've said yes in the past. I can only hope they don't take it personally. Perhaps it is that right now the pain in my head is lancinating and I'm not feeling very stable on my feet because of cervicogenic vertigo. My symptoms are different every day, so I can't even have the same elevator speech for every occasion.

Sometimes the most helpful and inclusive thing we can do for a disabled person in our community is to give them space and time to discover and explore their own capacities, especially if they have a new or progressive disability, rather than denying them opportunities or assuming we know what they should be capable of doing.

Rev. Diane Teichert: I am now the minister emerita of the Paint Branch Unitarian Church in Adelphi, Maryland, which I was serving at the time of my hemorrhagic stroke.

Initially, I was severely disabled. I couldn't sit up on the side of the bed, and I couldn't stand or walk at all. Bodily functions that require cooperation of muscles on both sides of the body were impaired, such as swallowing, reading, etc. But the plasticity of the brain is amazing, and I began to recover even before I was discharged from the Stroke Center to an acute care rehab hospital. I really was fortunate in the level of physical and occupational therapy that I received there. After I got out of the acute rehab care hospital, where I was for seven weeks, the church hired a minister part-time in a position they called interim caretaker minister. His instructions were to include me in the planning conversations and in the tasks of ministry as I became able, until such time as I was ready to decide if I could come back. So he and the three people on the Committee of Ministry met with me at my house monthly, seeing how things were going with me, seeing what I was actually like, which was a far cry from what I had been like. I lit the chalice in a service for the first time in the fall and preached with the interim caretaker minister in the winter. I dreamed of coming back only half-time and doing a shared ministry with somebody. I even found somebody who was interested, who I thought would be super, and we thought we could work together really well. Then about a year after my stroke, I concluded that this would be way too stressful and impede my continued recovery, and that the congregation really deserved to move ahead without me, find an interim minister, and then go into search for a new settled minister.

For me, this gradual decision-making process was great because I learned that people in the congregation really cared about me. Some were signing up to give me rides to my physical therapy and that kind of thing, and I think they felt good that they didn't just cut me off. From that standpoint, I really recommend it. I also have to be honest and say that there is a downside, and that is that just like I had a dream of coming back, some of them had a fantasy of my coming back, so delaying a decision for a year might have delayed their rejuvenation as a congregation. But how can you know what would have happened if another path had been chosen? It is really hard to say.

When someone is trying to judge whether someone else can do a particular thing, the question they are really asking is "Can they do this in the 'right' way?" We need to be aware of this tendency and not fall into it, because that is the wrong question to ask. It leads us to misjudge the person's capacity.

Often disabled people just need to be allowed to offer their contribution in a way that works for them.

Rev. Katie Norris: Normalizing neurodiversity means that we move away from this idea that people who are neurodivergent need to be managed to get them to fit into "normal" behavior and functioning. There is no normal. There are societal and cultural norms, which are all a construct. This idea that people need to fit into normal not only does not allow us to show up as our full selves, but our community misses out on many amazing and beautiful things we can learn from the diversity of our brains.

April Smith: Stereotypes about the capabilities of disabled individuals can work against full inclusion. In addition to a neurological condition that renders me disabled to some extent, I'm also neurodivergent. This means that I don't process information the way an "average" person would, and I sometimes struggle to communicate when I'm feeling intense emotions. But it doesn't mean that I don't deserve to have the same opportunities to participate as others. It just means that how I participate may look different than what is the norm. It's important to remember that each individual has unique abilities and needs and that presumptions can be harmful.

Mentally or emotionally disabled people are particularly susceptible to having their input dismissed as tainted by these conditions.

Rev. Katie Norris: Once you are public about certain mental health diagnoses, people perceive your behavior differently, especially when you raise concerns about group systems. There is a lot of stigma against our ability to lead and be in relationship with others. Many people attribute valid observations that we might have about life or organizational dynamics to our mental illness. For example, if we bring up that voices of some of the people in a meeting are being left out and ask how we can include them, our observation is often pegged as "too dramatic" or we're asked, "Do you think you feel that way because of your other issues?"

When congregations don't encourage and welcome the contributions of disabled people, any ableism they have internalized may be reinforced and a vicious cycle can begin, in which non-disabled people don't invite disabled people to participate and disabled people don't volunteer to do so. Giving people a role in the community gives them an anchor and a way to interact with others. Working closely with others is a great way to get to know them and build relationships that are not centered on the disability. Several people also told us that things they did within their congregation led them to life-changing opportunities outside it and a greater appreciation of their own skills and talents.

Kaden Colton: My deep involvement with local UU congregations, made possible by the use of Zoom during the pandemic, started with my founding of an LGBT spirituality group during the pandemic that I still run and led me to begin auditing courses at a local seminary in St. Paul. The first course I audited, Queer and Trans Theologies, deepened my understanding of my own spirituality and how to support others. And it got me interested in auditing other courses. I learned a lot and tried my best to practice what I learned with the LGBT spirituality group and in religious education workshops I cofacilitated.

My involvement at one of the congregations led to a minister inquiring if I would like to be on an internship support committee for a minister in training. I agreed and eventually ended up applying for the master of divinity in an interreligious chaplaincy program and began divinity school in January of 2023.

Kevin Wilson: I spent a couple of years attending service on Sunday, sitting in my nice comfortable pew in the back but not getting too involved in the community. I had found my home, but I was still nervous about getting involved and then losing that community. In 2018, I started running the sanctuary sound system every other Sunday. I felt at home behind the soundboard. I have always been comfortable with technology. Since I was a young child I have been using technology to navigate through the world. I remember having a laptop in school so I could take my own class notes, since my handwriting was difficult and hard to read.

I finally found my niche in my local church community. I became the tech guy. It wasn't long before I was getting phone calls from members asking for advice about how to fix a tech issue or which device would be a better buy. I felt happy and secure in my nice little corner of the world, but in the back of my mind I still felt like something was missing. I had been doing more research about what Unitarian Universalism was all about, and in my many hours of searching, I had discovered there were many different communities within the denomination to offer support. After doing a Google search, I found EqUUal Access.

After reading the EqUUal Access web page, I knew that I had found the support that I was missing. I remember attending my first EqUUal Access meeting. I was nervous. What if I said the wrong thing? Would they ask me to leave? I was welcomed into the community immediately, and I learned so much about the larger world of disability. More importantly, I found a place where I could go and share my experiences and frustrations.

Even more importantly, I had found a place where people were not ashamed of their disabilities; in fact, they embraced them. After attending several meetings of EqUUal Access, I began to lose my shyness and started speaking about my disability openly with others and pointing out accessibility issues. Then I got a phone call I never expected. My church asked me if I wanted to join the board of trustees. My initial thought was that I wasn't ready for this responsibility, but I knew it was time for me to break out of my comfort zone and take an active role in running the church.

My movement to the board of trustees came at an important time in world history. A few short months later, our world was changed forever by the COVID pandemic. Our congregation went from an in-person-only service to online-only overnight. From the beginning, my goal for online services was to make them accessible to as many people as I possibly could. It was a difficult road, but I was able to teach my congregation that accessibility was a goal that could be achieved. I attended General Assembly that year and became a member of the Disability Caucus. I don't think I got more than four hours of sleep, but it was the most productive week I had that year.

Through my work with the Disability Caucus, I was able to make a positive change in our denomination. My faith helped me find myself. My faith showed me that community could be a positive force for good. My identity as a person with a disability has allowed me to bring a unique perspective to my work and help make everything I do be accessible to as many people as possible and show the world that accessibility is a fundamental right.

Lisa Ferris: There are many disabled people out there who are willing to help, even willing to lead the way. We not only have the skills and knowledge to help make congregations more accessible but have gifts to offer in every aspect of UU life. We are teachers, accountants, computer programmers, tech folks, etc. We have material skills that can assist congregations. Some of us will be counselors and spiritual leaders. Instead of being fearful of what we will take from you, let us also give to you. When we are ignored and we spend all of our time trying to knock down the barriers preventing us from joining you, all of Unitarian Universalism misses out on a rich and vibrant community of people. It's all there for you if you will just unlock the doors.

Real inclusion isn't only about welcoming and enabling the participation of disabled people in an equitable way; it's also about honoring differences. A person's disability may in fact give them perspectives, experiences, and skills that non-disabled people are unlikely to have, and that could be real benefits to your community. For instance, disabled people often have particular insights into humility, the necessity of rest, empathy, resilience, interdependence, non-perfectionism, problem solving, creativity, and persistence. And some disabilities tend to pair with specific talents.

Kate Ryan: I need Unitarian Universalism, and Unitarian Universalism needs me. Disabled people bring unique gifts with them because we are used to doing things in different ways. We're used to figuring out how to access things, we are used to fighting for justice, we are used to doing things the hard way.

Autistic people are often gifted in memory, in music, and in enthusiasm and loyalty to the church. Someone in my congregation once told me that I always say what everyone else is thinking but no one is brave enough to say, such as pointing out a racist phrase or asking a question about what is going on. This is true. My disabilities have taught me that if I don't speak up, there is a good chance that nobody will. And it is my religious obligation to speak up for other marginalized groups because there are times when I cannot speak for myself and need others to do so for me.

Dana Snyder-Grant: I've had multiple sclerosis for forty-two years, all my adult life. I have a relapsing/remitting course, with flare-ups of double vision or leg weakness and spasticity or decreased coordination in my hands, all often accompanied by excessive fatigue. I worked as a psychotherapist, specializing in chronic illness and disability. I often say that MS is just like life, only more so. Before the MS, I had difficulty asking for help or trusting my own judgment or accepting limitations. These struggles came back to haunt me.

When my husband and I joined a local UU congregation a few years after September 11, 2001, many of us were seeking to find order out of chaos. Now here I was, engaged with a new community of seekers and travelers in a frightening world. I was not long from retirement age as a social worker, and I was drawn to the small group of five pastoral lay ministers. We are trained to accompany fellow parishioners who are facing life transitions such as job loss, illness, a death in the family, or another vulnerable space. I soon also joined the congregation's pastoral care choir, the By Your Side singers. Small groups of two to five sing for parishioners living in these liminal spaces, often of loss. I now assist the group's director with coordinating the choir, communicating with the singers and with families or facilities where parishioners receive care. Other singers may assist me with a ride or navigating a space, especially as the illness has progressed in me and is visible. With foot drop and compromised walking, I consider the MS to be more of a disability now. I still travel with other parishioners to our sings. Some days,

I may use a walker or a scooter to navigate. I may feel awkward when entering a facility with a walker or scooter and a nurse asks how she can help me.

I've asked myself if I can still offer pastoral care, even though one might consider me a "wounded healer." I like to think that the wounds I carry from MS might provide some comfort and assist others to open up and more easily accept their vulnerability. We all give and receive from one another all the time. Both singers and those we sing to experience healing from this practice. In general, the other singers, lay ministers, and parishioners offer me affection and respect. My involvement with the pastoral care singers is one of the most important and precious things I do in my life, meaningful to my sense of belonging in the congregation, to my larger purpose, and to my sense of wholeness. With this ministry and the work of our Commission on Institutional Change, of which I am a member, barriers have been broken down as we search for ways that our congregation may be unwelcoming and/or carry elements of white supremacy.

Imari S. Nuyen-Kariotis: I believe that disabled people can bring many gifts to their congregations. We are often creative, compassionate, and resilient. We can offer our unique perspective on faith and spirituality. Disability can be a source of strength and wisdom. People with disabilities often have to learn to be resourceful and creative in order to get things done. This can lead to a deep sense of self-reliance and confidence. People with disabilities often have to be resilient and strong in order to cope with the challenges of their disabilities. This can inspire others to persevere in the face of difficulty. People with disabilities can bring hope and joy to their UU congregations, showing others that it is possible to live a full and meaningful life with challenges.

We can also offer our talents and skills to help make our congregations more inclusive and welcoming. It's been a long hard struggle, but I believe that UU congregations can be a model for other faith communities on how to be inclusive of disabled people.

Helen Armstrong: I encourage all Unitarian Universalists to embrace disabled people with intersecting identities in our spaces. Seek out disabled people for our knowledge and ability to think about things flexibly. We have learned to be very resourceful and have lots of ideas and creativity. Be pleased with us!

Rev. Jennifer DeBusk Alviar: I have cultivated innovative strategies for navigating my executive functioning challenges. This is particularly true as a disabled minister specializing in eco-theology. For example, I frequently take photos during my daily nature walks. Photography offers me a visual aid and tracking device in capturing snapshot moments to process at my own pace without distraction or time pressure.

These multisensory inputs help me integrate and synthesize my ideas into a succinct, compelling message around ecotheology. Traditional preaching on a purely verbal level would not be possible. These visual, kinesthetic, experiential modalities provide the necessary traction in strengthening my skills around memory recall and information processing.

Disabled people are resilient and resourceful. They have the wisdom of their long experience dealing with limitations on what they can do, coming to terms with diagnoses and often traumatic change, discerning what's important to them, advocating for what's right, and speaking truth to power. That's wisdom any community can benefit from, and it can't be captured in an inspirational poster or personal interest story on the local news about a disabled person doing something that non-disabled people can do. The wisdom of disabled people is often so much richer and deeper, and it becomes available to us in relationship, in working together, in navigating a community together. When we enable access but don't build relationship, allow participation but don't listen, or insist on conformity, we miss out on learning what disabled people know through their life experience.

Rev. Barbara Meyers: My religion was perfectionism. Everything I did had to be perfect, and nothing I or anyone else did ever met these expectations. I went to school, got good grades, got a PhD in a scientific field, and worked very hard at my job, believing that I had to do it perfectly, and that other than my family, nothing else mattered in life. I was totally analytical, and I believed that life would be lived that way.

My first experience with psychiatry was shortly after the birth of my daughter in 1978. I had the perfect husband, perfect child, perfect job, perfect home, etc., but I couldn't live up to my own expectations and couldn't function. I wanted to die. My psychiatrist quickly stabilized me with a combination of drugs and psychotherapy, including a period of hospitalization. I was deeply disturbed by this experience. It was further indication of my lack of perfection. The other patients frightened me; they heard voices, saw visions, etc. I couldn't accept that I could be like these people in any way.

After several years of hating myself and having an essentially joyless existence, I sat down and took stock of my situation. In the end, I decided something had to change. I wasn't willing to live my life this way anymore. I didn't know how or what the change would be, but it had to happen, and I was willing to do anything required for the change. I started to go regularly to my psychiatrist to explore myself. I found this a difficult, emotional, and fascinating experience.

I'm telling you this to illustrate that a person can fundamentally change the way that they look at the world—even at the thing most feared, and that this can be a healthy change.

One of the most damaging aspects of the stigmatization of disabled people in faith communities is the presumption that they aren't capable of leadership and the refusal to even consider them for such roles. In fact, congregations have historically been more reluctant to consider disabled religious professionals than they have been to consider LGBTQ or BIPOC people, whose acceptance in these roles is recent and still sometimes fragile.

Rev. Keith Kron: In the Beyond Categorical Thinking workshops I led, participants were asked to identify any concerns they had about calling a minister with various identities. Even for the mid-nineties, the consensus of what was anonymously shared was shocking. There were concerns raised that the minister would be a single-issue minister, come with an agenda, and not be able to serve well. Participants shared beliefs that Black ministers would not be smart enough, that gay or lesbian ministers would make the congregation unsafe for children, and that disabled ministers would not have the stamina for the job.

When these anonymously collected concerns were shared, jaws dropped. People shifted uncomfortably in their chairs. Heads shook. Well at least they did in response to comments about race and ethnicity and sexual orientation. This was not the case around disability. In fact, the results around disability became fairly predictable.

Invariably, the following concerns were shared aloud:

The applicant won't be able to do the job of ministry or have the stamina to be able to do the job.

Our building isn't accessible and/or it will cost too much to make the building accessible.

We won't be able to understand the minister. Will they be able to communicate with us?

Will we have to take care of the minister?

Even when these concerns were shared, rarely did heads shake. Some congregants argued that these were legitimate concerns. Fortunately, others disagreed, though more often there was a silent majority not entering the conversation.

A few congregations pointed to their ramps as proof of their accessibility, and occasionally an elevator. But often there was a sense that a minister with a disability would be a burden, that the congregation wouldn't be able to cope, and that the majority of members would feel sorry for the minister.

Over two decades, concerns around gender, sexual orientation, and race and ethnicity waned and evolved, but the same concerns remained for disability, with the only difference being that mental health was added to the questionnaire after 2005 and not wanting a minister who was depressed became another leading concern, along with stamina, building accessibility, communication, and caretaking.

The workshop also changed. Case studies were added, based on actual events that had happened with ministers as part of the search process. Participants were asked to discuss in small groups how they would respond in these situations. They were asked, for example, what they would say to a member who said they just shouldn't get a minister who used a scooter because the building was not accessible and the cost to make it accessible was prohibitive and the minister would probably not have the stamina for the job.

The case study that got the most attention was of a minister who, during candidating week, was discovered by a member taking medication for depression. The minister asked the member not to tell anyone. And the workshop participants were asked what they would do in that case.

This case study produced a lot of bewilderment and avoidance. Often people said being asked to keep secrets was unhealthy. Others said that disclosing the information was unfair to the minister. In one congregation, this conversation took an interesting turn. Several participants got loud, insisting that the minister should reveal that they lived with depression and that the congregation had a right to know this ahead of time. There was growing agreement. Finally, a member of the Search Committee raised his hand. This was a retired doctor. He said, "I will gladly ask every applicant to share what medications they are on, and then share the candidate's medication with you." He paused then as people nodded their heads, and then he continued, "Provided each and every one of you tells me now what medications you are on." The room went completely silent. The Search Committee member spoke again: "You don't ask your coworkers what medications they are on. You don't ask your boss what medications they take. You don't ask your children's teachers what medications they take. And I can tell you as a doctor, a lot of doctors are on medication. Why are we creating a double standard for a minister that we don't have for anyone else?"

This was likely the quietest full minute I can remember having in nearly three hundred workshops. It continues to be a teaching story more than a decade later.

Pey Carter: Disabled people have the right to be involved in all aspects of church life, including teaching RE and being behind the pulpit. I withdrew from the ministerial process last year because I could not find a CPE site that would accommodate my needs and there wasn't an option for problem solving so I could be ordained. It hurt to see the seven years I put into that journey go down the drain. My ministerial internship was almost two hours away from where I lived, so I commuted two to three times a week for two years with a small stipend of a few hundred dollars. I attended seminary at more than full time, taking classes every quarter with no breaks. I spoke at the Mid-America Regional Assembly and presented at General Assembly.

Not being able to take the final steps toward ordination broke my heart, and it took quite some time to let go of the hurt and anger. I stopped guest preaching for about six months, and only just recently started going back to Unitarian Universalist services.

Some people are surprised I've gone to seminary or was able to do a ministerial internship as a disabled person. Almost anything is possible if there is support, accessibility, and inclusion.

Rev. Amanda Schuber: As I moved into my thirties and began to claim my disabled identity more openly, I wasn't as invisible, but I was afforded less agency to determine what I am capable of. "The committee felt that your disability was enough for you to handle right now. We didn't want to burden you with leadership responsibilities too." He said it with the deep caring concern of someone proud that they had shown such kindness. This wasn't the first leadership position I had been passed over for, and it wouldn't be the last. It had taken me fourteen years to claim this queer disabled body as my own, but in so doing, I had somehow opened the door for the assumptions of others about what I can and can't do to seep in.

Internalized ableism can make it difficult for disabled people to recognize their own leadership potential, which is why they should be actively encouraged to consider leadership.

Opportunities for leadership can be life-changing in a world that rarely sees disabled people as leaders, congratulating itself instead on merely (and minimally) including them.

Rev. Katie Norris: So much of how we are evaluated as ministers relies on neuronormative behaviors. Goddess help you if you are a minister with ADHD. We are often judged as uncaring, disrespectful, lazy, and just not willing to work hard, when in reality, some of us just have trouble with executive functioning.

I have a disability, but I knew it was never really okay to ask for an accommodation such as an administrative assistant in parish or community ministry to help with executive functioning tasks.

Being a neurodivergent minister also brought challenges for our son and his faith formation. My young son saw a dynamic where I was terrified to be myself, worried about being pegged as having "disruptive behavior," while at the same time he stood, knee-high, as a congregant screamed at me for changing an element in worship one Sunday for a special service. As a mother, I worried about what this was teaching my son, not only about our faith, but about how people who are neurodivergent are treated. Those of us with different neurotypes are held to a much higher standard than most people, and this does show up in our churches. It is especially prominent when we become lay leaders or ministers.

Unitarian Universalist leaders who become disabled or whose disability progresses during their tenure deserve as much support as possible to maintain their leadership roles through changing circumstances and capacities. Congregations need to recognize that even if the person can't do everything they used to do or do it in the same way they used to, they still have leadership experience and earned wisdom to share. People who are in paid positions when they become disabled may fear losing their job.

Rev. Michelle LaGrave: When I first began my ministry, I had fewer counts against me. I was a large, queer woman. The disability and the service dog came later. I was serving a congregation at risk of dying as its developmental minister. By my third year, I was experiencing a myriad of health issues and my mobility was rapidly decreasing. These were probably not unrelated to the also rapidly decreasing level of health in the congregation, which was already not in the best of shape. It was a tough ministry.

I had begun experiencing chronic pain, among other odd symptoms, and an orthopedist told me I should try to avoid using stairs as much as possible and signed me up for a disabled placard for my car. I started using a cane at times. I began seeing other doctors as well. One told me she would not be surprised if I eventually wound up with a diagnosis of multiple sclerosis. Just the year before, I had been doing well. I had marched in the Memorial Day parade as usual. And I had applied to be matched with a ministry dog, who would serve as a pastoral care assistant in crisis situations (I was also a volunteer fire chaplain) as well as in my congregation. When I finally received the call that I had been matched with a dog, after a full year's wait, I was in a much different condition. Once the professionals at the service dog agency witnessed how poor my mobility had become, they pretty much insisted I switch from a ministry dog to a service dog. My doctor agreed, my training with the service dog continued, the match happened, and I brought Bella home.

Meanwhile, the situation in my congregation had continued to deteriorate. While they continued to evaluate my ministry favorably, and I did move into full fellowship, they also severed my contract about a month and a half early. They said they wanted to save money, and they did. They no longer had to pay me for about four weeks of vacation or a trip to General Assembly.

To say that this was a difficult time is to put it mildly. I was newly identified as disabled, without clear diagnoses, struggling to understand and adjust to this new label, newly matched with a service dog, newly fully fellowshipped, newly hurt by the congregation I had been serving, and now newly unemployed—at least until my chaplain residency started in August. It was a lot. It's also one of the many stories about why we, as an Association, are now looking for ways to hold congregations accountable for their behavior, just as ministers have long been held accountable for ours.

And so it was that, after my first developmental congregation, a chaplain residency, and a congregation not ready to call a queer, disabled minister, I answered a call to interim ministry and became an officially accredited interim minister. It is a pull I still feel, and yet this kind of ministry is challenging in many ways. We haven't done the work we need to do as an Association, at least not yet, to support interim ministry. The choice to answer the call to interim ministry comes at a high cost: physical, financial, and emotional.

Interim ministers do not have the opportunity to earn sabbatical from any of our congregations. Although a sabbatical fund has been started within the UUA, I suspect it will be many years before it comes to fruition in any meaningful sense. Too little money is paid into it by our congregations, and with our search cycles the way they are, it would be challenging to take less than a full year off and still be able to find a ministry for the remainder of the year. Even worse, much of the vacation time we earn is used to move—to pack, unpack, and do all the chores related to moving. Moving is neither restful nor renewing, and it is certainly not vacation.

So we interim ministers are already short on rest and renewal and have ministered through an exhausting pandemic, the same as all the called ministers. Then when we do move, we have added and frequent costs: the recommended rate for moving expenses is $5,000 less for interim ministers than it is for called ministers. The moving reimbursement, especially when moving from state to state, doesn't cover all the costs, even when self-packing, plus it is counted as added taxable income, a not-inconsequential figure when moving every other year. Other costs and fees add up too. New car registrations, license plates, driver's licenses, outfitting new apartment configurations (size, shape of windows, bathrooms, etc.). Plus there is the added work of finding new care providers, changing addresses for everything, and coming out, over and over again, including in states where that doesn't feel safe. The physical, emotional, and financial tolls of interim ministry are high for everyone, even more so for someone who is disabled and queer.

Ensure Representation

Congregations must ensure authentic representation by prioritizing the inclusion of disabled people in leadership and staff roles. This not only creates a more equitable community but also enriches the congregation with diverse perspectives and insights.

Never underestimate the impact on disabled people of seeing other disabled people living authentically and openly in your community, contributing in the ways that work best for them, and being valued for their presence. For every disabled person taking their place as a leader, there are others watching and learning about your community's faithfulness to its values.

Representation is also about giving disabled people opportunities to share their lived experiences. For every disabled person who speaks about their experience, there are others who have had similar experiences they have not shared, but who long to have their perspective validated and given voice in the community. Creating opportunities for sharing multiplies and amplifies the message of care that you send, until it reverberates throughout your community. But an invitation to share should never be treated as an obligation to educate the congregation, which must take responsibility for its own learning.

Pey Carter: What keeps me coming back is the people and church leadership who are willing to hear the stories and experiences of disabled people with an open heart and mind and foster deeper discussions about topics people may find difficult.

Also, the impact of storytelling in our congregations and hearing a wide range of voices. Every time I share my experiences or ideas, there are always people who state things like they haven't seen a disabled person behind the pulpit or they never bothered to share their experiences because they thought no one would care.

I guest preach at different congregations, and it is wonderful when I hear that my sermon on disabilities has them thinking they are grateful to have me because they learned more than they anticipated.

It fills my spiritual and community buckets when people are accepting and want to learn so they can be better allies. When people say, "Wow—I hadn't thought about that," it makes a huge difference. When church leadership implements a request, like providing a larger font in an order of service or moving an item so that it is more accessible, that matters.

To other disabled Unitarian Universalists trying to find a home in our congregations: Don't be afraid to speak out and share your experiences. Congregations are a microcosm of society, which means that there are people in the congregation who can relate in some way to what you are going through. You are not alone or the only person struggling with health issues there.

Maria Zuccarello: My husband and I attended a service at Neighborhood Unitarian Universalist Church in Pasadena. By chance, we walked into the senior high service. Right away, I noticed one of the high schoolers used a wheelchair. Not only that, he seemed comfortable being in front of the group talking about himself. That impressed me. I'm always looking for positive representation of disability in a community. I do have a disability but I am not a wheelchair user. I have a facial difference and hearing loss as well as hydrocephalus and scoliosis. I have never encountered anyone with my unique mix of disabilities and rarely even with any one of them in my daily interactions. But representation matters.

Rev. Keith Kron: Gradually, as people became more aware of others who had an apparent and/or non-apparent disability, some of the ideas about disabled people changed. They changed more when participants knew more than two people with a particular disability.

Fully including disabled people in congregational life requires culture change, and disabled people can't drive culture change on their own. Asking them to try puts an undue burden on them to be the faces and voices of the full spectrum of disability life experience. It's also essential to carefully and intentionally curate (and often create) disability-inclusive material for worship services, religious education, small group ministry, reading groups, and other contexts.

In order to meaningfully represent disability, existing narratives must be reframed and harmful stereotypes challenged. Stories and images of disabled people should be incorporated into congregational publicity, educational materials, and other texts, depicting them not as tokens or heartwarming anecdotes but as everyday participants in community life who are valued for more than just their disability. Disability justice must be integrated into sermons, worship services, and congregational programming. Only by embedding disability awareness into all facets of congregational life and empowering disabled people can congregations create a welcoming and inclusive environment and truly embody our UU values.

IMPACTS OF ABLEISM

Whether you are disabled or not, we expect that all of you reading this book have known at some point how it feels to be isolated, left out, denied opportunity, dismissed, or treated as unimportant. If you are not disabled, we invite you in this section to consider the impacts of these types of experiences for people who endure them repeatedly, even in faith communities that proclaim their affirmation of everyone's worth and dignity and of compassion in human relations.

Internalized Ableism

Internalized ableism is the ableist beliefs and judgments that disabled people have absorbed through living in an ableist society, and which they may apply both to themselves and to others who share similar experiences. It can arise from a variety of internal and external factors, and each person experiences it differently. Negative societal beliefs about disability are often deeply ingrained, making them difficult to recognize in everyday language or behavior. The ways we talk about and respond to disabled people and the decisions that we make about how or whether to meet their needs or include them in our plans can perpetuate harmful stereotypes and promote internalized ableism. In addition to making people feel bad about themselves, internalized ableism can interfere with their ability to cope with the reality of their disability and practice self-care. Congregations have countless opportunities to work toward dismantling internalized ableism, starting with the essential first step of acknowledging its existence.

Rev. Diane Teichert: Internalized ableism enters into what we imagine we can do. And I definitely struggled with that. For example, my adult son really tried to encourage me to get a scooter. He said, "You'll be able to do so much more, Mom." But I had this mental image, an emotional image really, of people using scooters at General Assembly and me thinking judgmentally that if they just took care of themselves and lost weight, they wouldn't need a scooter. So here I am actually needing a scooter and I have these mental tapes that I've harbored in my head for as long as I was a minister. And then I realized that this is totally messed up. Where was I coming from, making that judgment? And I realized how it disabled me to have that old ableist tape in my head, maybe as much as my physical disabilities did. It was the function of ableism within me.

Dana Snyder-Grant: As I learned more about the spiritual teachings of Unitarian Universalism, found in our Principles, that we all have inherent worth and dignity within an interconnected web of being, they spoke deeply to me. I knew that our Third Principle, acceptance of one another, began with acceptance of myself. Acceptance by others of the disability within me encourages my own self-acceptance and transparency.

Isolation

Many disabled people are isolated in all areas of life. Sometimes their condition itself inherently makes it difficult to be around other people or manifest in behaviors that fall outside of the dominant culture's expectations. These behaviors are usually not intrinsically harmful to the self or others and the disabled person cannot control them easily, particularly in certain situations. One form of inflexibility that excludes disabled people is an insistence on maintaining an environment that others prefer at the expense of disabled community members' ability to be present as their whole authentic selves, comfortably and without having to make painful and stressful efforts to conform.

Gale Callaghan: Autism affects me most with social and sensory concerns. I'm not able to know when a conversation isn't interesting to the other party. I can't know how loud I am or if I'm talking too much. I experience physical pain when exposed to bright lights, loud sounds, or strong smells, even if they don't seem that intense for anyone else.

I was not able to attend services when I was younger due to my sensory needs. Asking a young teen to sit in an all-white room with a hundred adults in their seventies is already a tough ask without my need for visual input. And there were no classes or groups for anyone over fifth grade. To keep myself safe, I had a habit of pushing the sides of my eyes, which led to vision problems.

My community helped me with this by not requiring me to be in the sanctuary and instead was able to participate in congregational life by spending time in the nursery with very young children. Now, as an adult, I find that while I am more able to experience UU services in a more traditional way, the social expectations on me are much higher. It's no longer okay for me as an adult to rock my body or make sounds.

I understand best and am at my happiest when I'm not thinking about the expectations put on me by society.

Many people join a congregation because they are looking for community, and accessibility and inclusion are essential if that need is to be met. But disabled people often end up isolated within the community or even driven out of it. Sometimes they withdraw, either quickly or after a long period of trying, because the pain and the effort are just too intense.

Shelly Rohe: It is not okay to think that a disabled person does not need to be included if a committee meeting is not accessible. Hold the meeting in a place that is. It is hard to put into words the feeling of isolation and deep sadness at being left out because of something I can't help.

Penny Clipperton: When Ian was living in the group home, I went with him and his residential worker for his Sunday morning outing, which always took place at the food fair in Southcentre Mall. What a dreary place this is on a Sunday morning! The place is empty except for one section with half a dozen tables, each occupied by a disabled person, a dish of French fries, and a caregiver. The only visible interaction is those staff who are chatting on their cell phones. I was unimpressed, and I wanted so much more for Ian and for everyone there!

At that time, I was a member of the Raging Grannies, many of whom were Unitarian Universalists. I asked some of them if they thought Ian might be able to fit into a UU congregation and they said yes. On our very first Sunday, the service was about climate change, and it occurred to me how comforting it would be to belong to a community of people who share that concern. I thought, hey, this might have something to offer me too!

Liz Conejo: The first incident was when I approached the music director about the possibility of joining their house band. I'm highly confident in my musical skills/talents and, generally speaking, have a great deal to offer, but she couldn't be bothered and blew me off on the two occasions I asked!

I then heard about a UU project for helping newly arrived immigrants/refugees and volunteered to serve as an interpreter and/or help out with whatever was needed. My first language is Spanish and I too am an immigrant and fully understand the challenges of moving to a new country because I've lived it. Again, no response from the project leader.

At one of the group discussion meetings, I pointed out that although social justice, racism, LGBTQ, and immigration issues were important, disability-related challenges likewise needed to be addressed, but the group reacted with silent indifference.

The final rejection came at one of the monthly potlucks, when a couple of women approached to invite me to join their hiking group. I greeted them with a warm smile, introduced myself, and gladly accepted their invitation. I gave each of them my contact information, and that was the end of it.

I can count on one hand the individuals who have shown their support by providing transportation to/from social events, the ones who've made the effort of including and bringing me into their circle. I'm thankful and appreciate their sincerity and generosity.

A 2014 study by the British disability advocacy organization Scope found that 67 percent of people felt uncomfortable talking to a disabled person, and this discomfort primarily stemmed from fear, ignorance, and lack of exposure.[10] This discomfort can significantly contribute to the increased risk of social isolation that disabled people face.

---

10 Scope, "Brits Feel Uncomfortable with Disabled People," press release, May 7, 2014, scope.org.uk/media/press-releases/brits-feel-uncomfortable-with-disabled-people.

Charlie Farrell: I have dementia and now I live in a new world. I have short-term memory loss, which means at any moment I may lose a single word or several words, which causes me to stop talking.

How can I help? How can you help?

I can help by telling you that I have dementia and wearing a nametag with a small forget-me-not flower (the symbol for dementia) so that others know my name and what I have. This way people can know that I might need some help with conversations and need more time to process what people say.

You can help by saying hello and inviting me into the group. Do not isolate us! Isolation itself is a disease.

Katherine Rubie: Since the pandemic, I have been a shut-in. First it was because of the pandemic, and then when things started loosening up, I got diagnosed with stage 4 appendix cancer, which is a rare and incurable cancer. I really started off trying to have a positive attitude. But one thing I clearly experienced was a sense that people began avoiding me, even with Zoom allowing the congregation to continue meeting when in-person services were not possible for several people. After several months of being in that very positive mindset, I began to have doubts and I started feeling alone and isolated.

I started realizing that I kept ending up in the same breakout room with the same people every week. When I ended up in a different breakout room, everybody would suddenly leave so I was left in the room by myself. I'd have to go back to the main room to get reassigned to another room, the same room I always seem to be in. It was all starting to feel very hurtful.

For the last few months, I've debated withdrawing my membership from the congregation because overall, I'm not feeling supported. There are a handful of people who I have friendships with, but many people who I thought cared about me don't make any effort to contact me, and when commenting in the Zoom chat or on Facebook, they don't seem to respond to me.

A history of negative experiences in community and internalized ableism can cause people to doubt whether their presence and contributions are welcome, even if welcome is expressed. In order for the welcome to be felt, it must be active, proactive, and sincere. A newsletter announcement that "all are welcome" is nice, but it doesn't indicate that anyone has ensured that disabled people can actually participate. But an offer to give someone with mobility issues a ride extends welcome and shows that their presence is valued.

Part of being included in congregational life is having people know you as the precious person you are, notice when you are present, and miss you when you aren't. Some disabled people may not be able to attend as often as they would like. Or they may withdraw in the wake of negative experiences related to their disability in the community. Checking in with them to tell them that their presence was missed as a gift lets them know they are important to the life of the congregation.

Katherine Rubie: There are things the congregation has done that have been helpful, such as sending me two cards signed by various members of the congregation. For me, that is really a big deal. Sending me a card is everything. It tells me that people really are thinking of me, even if I don't get to say hi to them on Zoom or go anywhere or do anything with them. One member has come a couple of times with her dog for a bit of pet therapy. It's those kinds of things that make one feel good. When someone is willing to spend time with you, or to send a card, or to ask how you are in a breakout room, that means the world. Simple things make life so much more fun and worth engaging in.

Diana C. Archibald: My increasing absences after my Parkinson's diagnosis did not seem to spark any concern, apart from one friend at church who began to check on me from time to time, not to ask "How *are* you?" but to say she missed me and to suggest we go for a walk or a chat on the phone and catch up. Around this time, our parish minister and I began to have periodic conversations about the nature of hope. As it became easier and easier to skip church, my isolation from my faith community grew. Attendance at church is optional for Unitarian Universalists; nobody would ever dare interfere with individual freedom. Except for those stalwart volunteers who hold everything together. They absolutely must attend. But I wasn't at that level anymore. I suppose people were just thinking that I was a typical UU and not going to church was my own business. We don't ask, we don't pry, and we certainly do not talk to someone about their attendance. So it was either go to church and hear "How *are* you?" or not go to church and feel left behind.

I really do need help. But it is not the kind of help that is easy to request outright, like a ride to an appointment or a dentist recommendation. I need people to ignore outward appearances and check on me anyway. I need to feel missed if I am not present, not "out of sight, out of mind." I need to be recognized as someone who can still contribute, and whose participation is worth ensuring and enabling through accommodations. I need to feel like someone who is valued and, despite not being able to contribute sometimes, valued because I have inherent worth and dignity, and I am respected and loved just as I am. I need to belong to something bigger than me and my disease, to feel like I am part of an important collective effort. And I need naps.

I wish I could tell them that's what I want. Not pity but community. Not freedom for me to do my own thing, including not attending church, but outreach to bring me back.

Penny Clipperton: I feel so happy and excited when I see and hear people warmly greeting Ian on Sunday mornings when he attends or asking after him when he doesn't.

At Calgary, Ian is noticed when he is here, known for who he is, and missed when he is absent. He is recognized and appreciated. So many of the congregation have offered these gifts, including, in particular, music director Jane Perry, when she announces, "Ian is in the building!"

When Ian is in the building, he loves the music and the candles and the people. He loves to watch Ronnie Leah and Dorothy dancing in the aisles or get a head massage from Bernie. Once when he was noisy during the service and had to leave, chorister Susan Stratton admonished me. "Listen," she said, "when I am in the choir, I like to sing to Ian, and I can't do that when you take him out!" Rev. Debra has described to me her appreciation when he sometimes punctuates what she is saying with a sound of approbation. I loved it when Ben remarked, "He is attracted to Spirit." And when we joined in Liz's compassionate cooking work party, Joan said, "It was nice to have his spirit here."

Guided by our values and by respect for every person's inherent worth and dignity, UU congregations can do better than the world at large, extending welcome and connection to people who have trouble finding it elsewhere. It is, after all, what our congregations promise in signage and websites and outreach materials. We have an obligation to make that promise real.

Cumulative Microaggressions

There is a kind of trauma that results not from major devastating events or situations but from the steady drip of small negative interactions that pool together over time to create a tide of hurt and despair. Congregations have a fundamental mission of offering hope. To the extent that they contribute to that despair in anyone, they are failing in their mission.

Lisa Ferris: If it was only the door, I think we could have managed it. But many other things became as much of a barrier as the locked door. It was a little bit like death by a thousand paper cuts—isolated incidents don't individually seem that dramatic, but taken collectively, they wore us down.

Exhaustion and Disappointment

Having to navigate obstacles and argue about everything you need just to participate is a barrier to the spiritual benefits of religious community, making it just another place of struggle. Over and over again in the stories that disabled people sent in for this book, we see them taking pains to be understanding and patient about the complexities of accessibility. As much as we support this approach, it's also important to recognize that this is emotional labor that disabled people are expected to perform in all aspects of their lives just to achieve basic access and inclusion. As often as their requests are met with understanding, good will, and intentional inclusion, they are at least as often met with dismissal, inflexibility, and even hostility. Individual encounters with ableism may range from very minor to very serious, and the impact of them on the disabled person adds up.

Empathy calls us all to understand that people do not ask for accommodations, request help, or point out ableism in a vacuum. They do so in the context of every other way they have had to struggle in their lifetime and perhaps even that day. And every response to them is received in that context. Holding this reality can help communities to pay more attention to helping and not causing harm than to the convenience of the majority or its discomfort with changing "the way things are done."

Kate Ryan: The thing about autistic memories is that for us, incidents don't fade. Although I don't have the eidetic memory that some of my peers do, I do have a very good one. And so I remember. I remember, but I wish I could forget. . . .

I wish that I could forget sitting in a minister's office, being told that I was causing discord by holding people accountable for their actions. I wish I could forget being told that if I tried harder, I could understand someone's accent and follow the Spanish in the hymnal. I wish I could forget people complaining about my lack of eye contact, despite my being openly autistic. I wish I could forget a woman glaring at me, thrusting her arm out to stop me, and angrily saying "shhh!" at a workshop when I asked too many questions.

Rev. Amanda Schuber: For years, I was uncertain about my place in the sacred space of the church. I was required to spend so much energy focused on the near constant drip of reminders about accessibility that I found it hard to connect to the Divine. Building spaces that could accommodate me and others took so much from me that I had little left for deeper spiritual questions.

Lisa Ferris: Because of some personal, health, and job shenanigans in my life at the time, I found myself working four part-time jobs.

I needed to lose one. I chose to quit the UUA AIM project, even though I really thought my colleagues were first-rate and the project was an important one. I was just exhausted and disheartened by the Unitarian Universalists. It had been a decade, and those thousand paper cuts were really starting to burn. And now I saw them everywhere on a national level and it was really quite overwhelming. When I quit working for the UUA, I pretty much faded out of the church altogether. It was too tiring, and as a Deafblind person, I also had to advocate for myself in healthcare, in my children's education, in my career, and in just walking down the street being Deafblind. It was exhausting. Dealing with the Unitarian Universalists was optional; the others often weren't.

Marginalization and exclusion are painful in any community, and when they occur in religious communities, they cause a particular kind of heartbreak. Disabled people come to Unitarian Universalist congregations for the same reasons anyone goes to any faith community: to search for truth and meaning, pursue their highest values, and celebrate and grieve the twists and turns of their lives with people with whom they are spiritually aligned. So it's important for congregations to be aware of ways that they fail to include certain people, and thus fail to meet their spiritual needs.

Kate Ryan: Unitarian Universalism has a massive ableism problem, and for far too long, only disabled people have been doing anything about it. This has absolutely got to stop, but I honestly do not have the energy anymore to fight for what is rightfully mine.

Maria Zuccarello: As I dived deeper into church activities, I tried to bring disability awareness and activism where I could. As I understood it, Unitarian Universalism is faith in action. So I taught spiritual education classes and presented about disabilities to the volunteer teachers. I participated in services revolving around disability or mental health, urging awareness and action. I tried to rally church members to complete the Accessibility and Inclusion certification offered by the UUA. This at least resulted in creating an accessible, gender-inclusive restroom in a convenient spot for people who need it at our church. I worked with staff at our church to simply post our accessibility offerings on the church website. I hoped that would convey more dignity to more people with disabilities interested in the church. My most recent attempt at bringing disability to the foreground of people's attention was to participate in the Share the Plate Committee. Here I tried to steer attention to donating money to nonprofits focusing on the disability community. My hope was that in doing so, this would spark people's interest in issues people with disabilities face on a sociopolitical level.

I have had moments of fulfillment, of being heard. My worldview has been seen as worthy in this congregation. I can't deny that. At the same time, I learned something about the UU church. The ideals of the organization to work for a better world and to dismantle a whole slew of -isms (racism, sexism, classism, even ableism, to name a few) in the community at large must "start at home." UU members working for change inherently need to look within themselves and those working with them in this important project, to dismantle -isms within themselves and each other with love and kindness.

Often the experience of disabled people in congregations is mixed, with individual members being intentional about inclusion and ensuring access but no commitment being made by the community as a whole. Thus it is important not to leave the work of inclusion to individual efforts but rather to collectively challenge ableist frameworks and be collectively accountable as a community where disabled people are fully embraced and empowered with consistency.

Rev. Katie Norris: My journey being neurodivergent in the church, as a church member and as a minister, has been amazing and a struggle at the same time. At times, the stigma and oppression have been just heartbreaking for me.

When I first found Unitarian Universalism, I felt more acceptance than in other groups. I was raised Catholic, and there were so many rules about behavior and how you have to act in order to be accepted and loved. In Unitarian Universalist churches, it was more acceptable to be different, and I loved that. And yet I still felt like my difference was just different enough that it was still not okay.

April Smith: Unitarian Universalist congregations aim to create a welcoming and inclusive environment for all individuals regardless of their race, gender, sexual orientation, socioeconomic status, or ability. For neurodiverse and disabled individuals, however, ableism and microaggressions can still be prevalent in these spaces. It's time to move forward together from narrow definitions of our values and empty proclamations to a faith community that is focused on taking measurable actions to ensure accessibility and equality for all.

Unfortunately, disabled people often grow disillusioned in—and with—Unitarian Universalist communities. Our message is a powerful promise to people whose contributions and lived experience are regularly dismissed by the world at large, and when that promise is broken it can be heartbreaking. Painful experiences in one community, especially when they occur over and over again no matter how hard the disabled person tries to advocate for themselves, can lead the person to abandon Unitarian Universalism and all it could have offered them.

L. A. Wright: My parents had joined this congregation so I could receive a religious education embracing values and beliefs they held. The faith I was taught was that bigotry and oppression are wrong. However, in addition to the curriculum that taught about equality and justice, I learned that even in my church I was invisible.

In the mid-1960s, I was a member of the youth group, Liberal Religious Youth. Most of the activities planned by the advisors were sports-related: ski trips in the winter, ball games in the summer. No one seemed to notice or care that I could only attend on rare occasions when the activities included discussion groups or planning a youth worship service.

Lisa Ferris: In the ten years that I participated in Unitarian Universalist congregations and activities, my family and I faced a lot of locked doors—both real and metaphorical. We worked hard to open them. Sometimes we had success, sometimes we did not. Sometimes it even seemed as if our work only caused the doors to get additional, sturdier locks. After years of this exhausting work, slowly my family gave up. I was the last to hold out, but finally I didn't know why I was there anymore either. This is my story of being a UU failure, and how the UU church failed me.

I just didn't understand how to "be" in the church, nor how to take seriously what they proclaimed. This is the church that believes in the inherent dignity and worth of each person. This is the church that promotes justice, equality, and interdependence. This is the church that promotes acceptance of one another. To see these Principles proclaimed over and over and yet to feel like there is no place for you in this church hurts. To have worked so hard to try to help the church become welcoming and to be cast off as unimportant hurts. It hurts a lot.

Rev. Michelle LaGrave: Our Unitarian Universalist congregations, at their best, are lifesaving, life-affirming communities of refuge. This is no exaggeration. People who have been marginalized socially, politically, and economically can find among us not just a feeling of welcome or acceptance but an experience of true belonging, perhaps for the first time in their lives. Here, ideals reign supreme. This is a lot of what attracted me to Unitarian Universalism in the first place.

When these ideals are lived out well, we have the beginnings of beloved community and that is a beautiful thing to witness and be a part of. The problem comes when we don't live out our ideals well, or even at all. In those cases, our congregations can become places of heartbreaking disappointment. This has been my experience more than once. Though I shouldn't say it's just our congregations. Sometimes it's our Association, or our collegial circles, that hurt and disappoint.

When thinking about the impacts of ableism, remember that the experiences a disabled person may have in your congregation are never the whole story. They are added to the total of that person's life experience living and moving through the world with their disability. And if a person holds multiple marginalized identities, ableism may be only one layer of the oppression that shapes their world.

Rev. Michelle LaGrave: I am a person with a certain amount of privilege. I am a white, cisgender woman who is highly educated. Though I grew up in a mixed working-class home, I am now solidly middle-class. And I am a Unitarian Universalist minister, a role that comes with both power and privilege as well as a commonly used honorific, Reverend. I also hold identities that are marginalized. I am both queer and disabled.

Not being seen for who I truly am happens often in my queerness too. I am married to a trans man. He had been assigned female at birth and identified as a butch lesbian when we met, but that never felt quite right to him. He had the courage to transition shortly before we were married. I am fully in support of his transition and would never wish it otherwise, because witnessing him become more fully himself was such a beautiful thing. And the reality is that once he began to live his more authentic life, my queerness became hidden. We "pass" without wanting to as a heteronormative couple, even though our identities and much of our cultural life are queer.

Sometimes these hurts and disappointments are relatively small. I've been lectured by a UU elder who told me never to refer to myself as queer, that that was a horrible thing to call myself. And I've been laughed at when I shared that on some days it hurts to wash my hair. They thought I was joking. I was not. On bad days, shampooing can feel like a thousand needles piercing my scalp.

At other times, the hurt and disappointment have risen to the level of full broken-heartedness. This was the case when I once candidated for a called and settled ministry. It was a disaster. There were warning signs along the way, of course, though they came too late to make a difference. The Search Committee didn't seem to have a whole lot of enthusiasm in the way they presented me to the congregation. They put a massive amount of written information up on their website for the congregation to peruse on their own rather than highlighting anything in particular. During the actual candidating week, my spouse was cornered by a member of the congregation who quizzed him about why I hadn't told earlier that he is transgender. (This was in the written materials and the Search Committee was well aware.) I also found out during candidating week that the new policy of nondiscrimination in hiring that included gender identity, and which the Search Committee had earlier highlighted as a proud accomplishment, had only passed by 51 percent.

The final test came, of course, with the congregational meeting and vote at the end of the week, after I had preached a second time. The vote failed. When they spoke with me later, the interim minister and two members of the Search Committee all separately shared the same story. The congregational discussion was all about me being queer, being married to a transgender person, being disabled, being partnered with a service dog, and being large. My heart broke. This was the explicit conversation the congregation had had. No unconscious bias here. It was all laid out right there. I was shocked. Did anyone speak up and say that there was anything inappropriate about the discussion being all about my identities? I don't know. If it happened, no one has ever said so to me.

The world as it is came crashing in on me that day. And so I had a choice to make. After taking a deep breath (I didn't have much time, as I was about to be unemployed), I chose to double down and applied to become an interim minister. My new mission? My new calling? To adventure boldly around the country, teaching congregations through my authentic presence that it was okay to have a minister like me. If doors were shutting ahead of me, I would open doors behind me.

Rev. Amanda Schuber: "Yeah, but you're not, like, really disabled," she said. It wasn't the first time I had heard this. In fact, I had heard some variation of it so often that I was starting to believe it was true. After years of doctor's visits, blood draws, and navigating a healthcare system that tells women that pain can only be because of their weight or depression, I had finally been diagnosed a few months earlier with a nerve condition. I was twenty-five years old and had just moved to Boston from my home in the deep South to work at UUA headquarters. I didn't grow up Unitarian Universalist, but I had become deeply involved in the young adult community, largely in response to coming out just a few years earlier. I desperately needed a space to grow into my identities, to feel safe and seen, but I was finding it harder and harder to navigate spaces where I wasn't "enough": not UU enough, not queer enough, and certainly not disabled enough.

It is important to remember that disabled people, like everyone else, are not exempt from learning how to be good allies themselves; everyone has room to grow and learn when it comes to supporting marginalized communities.

Rev. Amanda Schuber: Despite my frustrations, I realize that I'm privileged. I live in a white body as a cisgender woman, and my ability to pass as straight and able-bodied allows me freedoms that are denied to many others.

Disillusionment can be compounded by the challenges of finding a congregation that is aligned with one's core beliefs and values. For disabled people, finding one that is also accessible adds another layer of challenge.

Kaden Colton: There were seven different Unitarian Universalist congregations in the Twin Cities Metro Area when I moved there. I wasn't entirely sure how I might be able to attend some of them. My knowledge of the public transportation system was quite limited. I explored the three I could access most easily and that were no more than an hour away via public transportation. This meant that I attended two of the larger congregations in person for a few weeks each. I was trying to get a feel for each congregation and if it would be a suitable fit for me. The pandemic lockdowns came into play less than two months after I arrived in Minnesota. Zoom made it easier to check out congregations that were further away. I could also connect with my last congregation, South Valley Unitarian Universalist Society, back in Utah. I felt comfort in being able to attend a service and be in community with people I had connection with, a spiritual community close to my own heart. I liked the messages I heard at these specific congregations.

The extra programming these two congregations provided throughout the week made it easier for me to connect with people in these congregations. These connections lessened my sense of isolation during the pandemic.

Lisa Ferris: We changed churches and started going to a much larger UU church in the downtown area. Some things were instantly better here. They had assistive listening devices that mostly actually worked. At the old church, they were either broken, low on battery power, or those speaking refused to use the microphones. The new church had Braille orders of service and large-print and Braille songbooks. Instantly, we felt like we were considered and that we were welcome. There were a few people who were genuinely kind to us. But the luster soon faded to a gray confusion.

On one of our first visits, a congregant came up to us and wanted us to join his group for disabled Unitarian Universalists. We were delighted. He was also vision and hearing impaired and was struggling to fit in. We also met another man who used a wheelchair. This man had also formerly gone to a smaller church. He said he quit going when he had gone to an evening event and had to knock on several windows before anyone would open the accessible door and let him in. ("Ah! That is familiar," I shared.) He told a story about how he was out in the cold and rain and was literally getting ill waiting and pounding on the basement windows while his wheelchair got stuck in the mud. That was his final straw at that church. We met and exchanged all kinds of ideas about how to make the church more welcoming to parishioners with disabilities. All of us had stories like these, and all of us sensed this defensiveness that occurred when we talked to the powers that be in the church about these issues. Most importantly, all of us had tried to find community and make friends but, although people were rarely openly mean, most barely said more than "hi" to us.

We decided that our approach should be more proactive. Instead of waiting for things to become problems and then be constantly put in the position of complaining, the Disability Committee, which we had invented on our own, would serve the church by helping it to become more accessible. We could do an accessibility audit and suggest changes to be made, and when disabled people had an accessibility issue, they could come to us and we would help them work it out. We would also offer educational programs and events for the church and invite them into our world with fun events. We were excited to take this on. All we needed next was to make it official with the endorsement and support of the minister and board.

We couldn't even get a meeting. Months went by, and the minister was always too busy to meet with us and finally told us it wasn't a priority at this time. Even though essentially we would be doing all the work, they didn't want us to proceed. They felt it was too much of an undertaking. They were not even willing to put a blurb in the newsletter saying that we were a committee that could help with accessibility concerns. There was only so much we could do on our own.

Several of the disabled people who sent in stories for this book told us of looking long and hard for a spiritual home that aligned with their beliefs, only to be relegated to its margins, or of finally having found a congregation where they felt they belonged, only to have to leave it and encounter heartbreaking disappointment at the next UU congregation they tried.

Liz Conejo: I'm a sixty-six-year-old woman who is totally blind. During a low point in my life, a dear friend invited me and encouraged me to attend the UU Church of the Verdugo Hills. She assured me it would be a most interesting, unique experience, and she was right!

I really didn't know what to expect, yet went in with an open heart and open mind. It was the first UU church I'd ever attended, and I had some concerns.

Everyone welcomed me with sincere warmth and friendliness, which took me by surprise.

Just the same, I braced myself for the other shoe to drop; you know, "Here comes the Jesus Squad!" and they're gonna try to shove religion down my throat. However, nothing of the kind ever happened, so I was able to relax, breathe, and enjoy this new experience.

Almost immediately, the director approached me and invited me to let him know how they could best accommodate my needs. He also encouraged me to let him know of any/all accessibility challenges that might likewise affect my overall experience.

Soon after, I logged onto their website and was pleased to find that it was indeed 100 percent accessible and usable. I couldn't help but smile contentedly like the Cheshire Cat!

At one of the Sunday post-meeting receptions, the director proposed the idea of having congregants lead a discussion on relevant topics each month, so I jumped right in, and offered a discussion on ableism, which was enthusiastically received by everyone.

I soon found myself wanting to attend regularly, and I did! I happily participated in several activities whenever possible, such as knitting for the homeless, giving money to the Social Justice Committee, and putting together personal care packages for the unhoused.

Again, my blindness was never a problem for anyone, and for the first time in a very long time, I felt a deep sense of connection and belonging.

If/when someone had a question about how I accomplished something, they would simply ask! If I didn't have an answer, we'd work it out, find a way, and get on with the business of making it work.

After about a year of bliss with the UUCVH, and due to circumstances beyond my control, I had to leave the Los Angeles area last fall and start a new life in a new area. I found and began attending the local congregation there.

My reception was tepid at best, and I couldn't help but notice the differences; this congregation was larger—about one hundred or so attendees, as opposed to the more intimate setting of the approximately twenty individuals I had come to see as my family, my people.

I jumped right in, seeking social connection, fellowship, and opportunities for community involvement, but I was met with subtle and not-so-subtle resistance from these supposed "progressives."

It was heartbreaking and bittersweet having to leave my home church, yet I didn't think twice about walking away from this one!

No one should have to struggle to be included, so yes, I leave the UU community with a bad taste in my mouth.

MEETING SPIRITUAL NEEDS

Disabled people have the same spiritual needs as everyone else. But their need may be particularly intense, because they are living in a world that isn't designed for them and does not recognize their full selves. Living with a disability confers profound spiritual learnings and also raises questions about identity, agency, meaning, purpose, and hope. People with sudden-onset or progressive disabilities are also on the spiritual journey of coming to terms with a prognosis, a changing life, and uncertainty about the future. They need a spiritual community that can hold all of that, and our communities are failing them if we deny them full access to what we have to offer.

Diana C. Archibald: One would think I would know the state of my ableness, but I can't seem to make up my mind. As a good Unitarian Universalist, I entertain too many questions in my free and responsible search for truth and meaning; I am ambivalent and indecisive. How much of my identity is now based on being a person with Parkinson's? What can I do to contribute to my family, my church, my community, my workplace? How do I embrace my time in this liminal space of in-betweenness, until this disease answers the question of disability for me?

Shelly Rohe: When I was told I would be paralyzed on my right side and never walk again, I wanted a peaceful, spiritual place to contemplate all of this where I could be around people but not necessarily have to interact with anyone. I needed a place where I felt safe. I chose the local Unitarian Universalist church. I had grown up Christian and had been looking for a church where I could feel welcome, even with all of my questions. The local UU church had a wheelchair symbol on their website, so I thought that, at the very least, they had considered disability in some way.

When I first ventured out to church I had limited knowledge of Unitarian Universalism, but I soon found myself among a mix of people who held differing beliefs yet were united in love. I was able to adjust to my new congregation in my own time, never once feeling pitied because of my disabilities. I have never looked back. It has been this acceptance that has empowered me to say yes to opportunities rich in experience again. It has been because of the love and support of my congregation that I can live life on my own terms.

We have so much to offer when we live up to the promise of our values. Religious communities can believe in people and give them acceptance and love, even when they don't believe in themselves. Indeed, these may be central factors in how well a person recovers from a temporary disability or lives with a permanent one.

Maria Zuccarello: Our reality is not always honored in the non-disabled world and is still a work in progress. For this reason, what stood out to me about the UU church was the First Principle: the inherent worth and dignity of every person. So I, a woman with a disability, matter. My experience, worldview, talents, and needs as a person with a disability are honored in this church. Each Principle after that is really just an elaboration of the same theme—worth and dignity.

Rev. Tandi Rogers: Many people with FASD [fetal alcohol spectrum disorder] are adopted. Many in my age group or older are the result not only of addictions but also of the lack of abortion options. We were not just swimming in alcohol but also swimming in trauma, shame, and violence. These can be residual. Religious community can be so healing with spiritual practices of belonging.

Rev. Barbara Meyers: When I started going to a Unitarian Universalist church in Hayward shortly after being released from a psychiatric hospital, I didn't tell anyone but the minister about my hospitalization. Even though they didn't know about my illness, the people in the church showed me many kindnesses; they involved me in church projects; they liked the bread I would bake for coffee hour and told me so; they were interested in my ideas. In other words, they treated me with compassion. They offered me ways that I could explore my emerging spirituality, searching for what was meaningful and true in my life. If those last few words sound familiar, they should. They come from the Unitarian Universalist Principles. Those people in that church lived out their religion to a very wounded person and it helped me to heal. They helped me to understand that people who have been hospitalized for psychiatric problems are all God's children. Even me. It changed the course of my life, and I am eternally grateful. I feel very fortunate to have found a safe place where I could explore my new spiritual feelings. This was enormously healing for me. I learned to balance my life with both rationality and emotion, something I had never done before. It was as if I had been wandering around lopsided for several years and was now centered. I began to be spontaneously happy.

In looking back at my illness, I believe I was living life without any spiritual outlet. I was trying to be perfect at everything and living my life by the principles of science alone. Now I'm just being me—getting to know who that is and liking her. It is an adventure, a journey that I will always be on.

Rev. Katie Norris: There is something about being in a community that is so open-hearted and understanding of neurodiversity that makes you feel not just technically seen. It's actually a religious experience, for me, to see people being themselves, supporting others, and using their gifts as a group to create something larger than themselves as individuals. For me, it creates that feeling of being connected to the divine.

Affirming Theology

Unitarian Universalism's theology that places love at the center of our values and affirms the inherent worth and dignity of all people, interconnectedness, compassion, and justice can resonate deeply with the life experience and spiritual needs of disabled people, many of whom come to us out of other traditions that preached more harmful beliefs related to disability. For some, the disability itself or the challenges of living with disability in our world can cause a crisis of faith. With our commitment to support the individual quest for truth and meaning, we can provide a place for people to find their spiritual grounding in alignment with their lived experience.

Lisa Holcomb: I've only been attending a UU church for five years, but my mostly invisible disabilities have been with me since I was a young girl. As an adult, I have many diagnoses, but as a child, I only had words for what felt wrong in my body or made me feel "other" compared to my peers. I spent years telling my parents and doctors what was wrong with me, only to have tests show there was nothing wrong. Being constantly told by experts that it was all in my head, I lost faith in my ability to interpret my body's sensations long before my heart lost faith in a God who was supposed to, but failed to, take care of me.

In other faith traditions, theologians of disability are also questioning and critiquing the idea of a broken world or that all people must adhere to an ideal body and/or mind to be "saved." These theologians, such as Nancy Eiesland, Rabbi Julia Watts Belser, and Dr. Amos Yong, among many others, are reshaping theological discourse by centering the lived experiences of disabled people and challenging ableist assumptions within faith traditions. Their work breaks down narrow definitions of wholeness, value, and perfection, advocating for a theology that celebrates human diversity and interdependence. By criticizing traditional notions of independence and "normal abilities," they affirm that disabled people contribute meaningfully to spiritual and communal life. Theologies of disability benefit everyone by fostering inclusive communities that embrace mutual care, challenge systemic injustices, and expand understandings of God. These perspectives help people break from rigid, exclusionary ideals, creating a faith practice that is richer, more compassionate, and accessible to all.[11]

---

11 See, for instance, Nancy Eiesland, *The Disabled God: Toward a Liberatory Theology of Disability* (Nashville: Abingdon Press, 1994); Julia Watts Belser, *Loving Our Own Bones: Disability Wisdom and the Spiritual Subversiveness of Knowing Ourselves Whole* (Boston: Beacon Press, 2023); and Amos Yong, *The Bible, Disability, and the Church: A New Vision of the People of God* (Grand Rapids: W. B. Eerdmans, 2011). Significant Unitarian Universalist disability theologians include Rev. Barbara Meyers, Rev. Suzanne Fast, Rev. Julián Jamaica Soto, and Rev. Naomi King.

Small Group Ministry

Small group ministry creates opportunities for deepening connection that are often more accessible than congregation-wide events and less intimidating for people accustomed to being shunned or judged because of their disability. And small groups help disabled people to be truly known beyond their disability and cultivate the relationships that can ground authentic, honest conversations about getting their physical and spiritual needs met.

Dana Snyder-Grant: One way in which I have felt both empowered and vulnerable in having a disability within the congregation has been in the telling of my story to the Tuesday group, a monthly gathering of parishioners who are sixty-five years and older. This group has a norm that fosters listening and vulnerability, in an effort toward growing resilience. UUs may sometimes find comfort with the intellect; we may be more circumspect with our emotions. The Tuesday group is a bit different, composed of an older population who may safely let down their guard. As we age, we may have similar experiences to those with disability—of loss, integration, and redefining our lives. I was encouraged by the other lay ministers to speak of my decision to stop driving, how I landed there at the young age of sixty-three. Two car accidents had led me to realize that my disabilities from MS interfered with safe driving. I spoke from a vulnerable place and in a space that embraced difference with congregants who had also begun to wonder how long they would drive. The Tuesday group offered me a safe forum to share learnings—that I remained whole and worthy, despite this chosen loss of what felt like an essential task of daily living. Mind you, this was not an easy journey. I had my low moments around not driving. You know—loss of independence and spontaneity. I shared spiritual reflections—that

I needed to let go of my ego and not take the loss personally, that asking for help could bring me closer to others, and that I could sit with ambiguity and grief in the body.

I don't believe I could have had these realizations without the support and understanding of the Tuesday group. Their request allowed me to see my decision as a valid one, which empowered me. The lay ministers, who encouraged me to offer this program, knew, along with members of the Tuesday group, that while the body may change, our hearts and spirits remain whole within us and help healing.

Kelly Riedesel: We have a grief group. Most of the folks who are in it are there because they lost a spouse. I'm fairly sure I'm the only person who's there because of disabilities and the grief of everything I deal with. That group is relieving. It's a balm because it's a place where I don't have to hold everything in. It's too much to hold all the time. There is also a writer's group. It is relieving and interesting to hear other people's responses to the prompts. It gets me out of my own head.

Ginny Vaughan: I think some people at church who do not know me cannot get past my physical disability. They do not know how to relate to me. This is why I joined small groups and ministry teams—so people could get to know me in a small situation. I intentionally joined the ministry teams so that members could see me working on an issue that I am passionate about.

Spirituality and Neurodiversity

There are many different ways for human brains to function. The idea that there is no "right" or "wrong" way to process information or to form and express ideas is intricately aligned with the Unitarian Universalist idea that people should be affirmed in their individual quests for spiritual truth and meaning. Unfortunately, people whose neurotypes don't conform to the standard are frequently perceived as not being very spiritual. This may be because they avoid eye contact with others, express emotion in unusual ways, do not communicate in spoken words, or have other unfamiliar or unexpected ways of interacting. It may be because they have difficulty sustaining attention in certain environments or when ideas are presented in a certain style.

Penny Clipperton: My son is a practicing member of the church. He participates in a shared expression of feeling and fellowship. There is a power in the united presence of shared community, and it is clear that he, who lives in the moment and is a master at reading nonverbal behavior and body language, responds to that power and that he relishes the sense of belonging that our congregation provides.

Before the COVID pandemic, Ian attended Sunday services and participated at Pride parades, Dances of Universal Peace, Halloween dress-ups, laughter yoga, dinners, social justice protests, and other events. When he moved into his own supported living house, many of the congregation attended his housewarming. Now, during the pandemic, we attend services by Zoom, as his conditions make him especially vulnerable to COVID. The two of us also attended Zoom choir practices, where all can join in with abandon, given that the participants can't hear each other anyway. He loves it when, at Sunday services, we all turn to the camera and wave a welcome to attendees in "Zoomland." And we all look forward to the day when Jane Perry can once again announce, "Ian is in the building!"

Five and a half years since he became a member, Ian continues to be a vital, loved, and loving presence at Calgary Unitarians.

The truth is that all people are spiritual beings, no matter how they express their spirituality or don't, or how they engage with worship. There is great variety in how both disabled and non-disabled people express and receive spiritual ideas. Universal design principles can serve us well here, calling us to engage different learning styles regardless of whether they are typically called "disability." Congregations can and should offer content in multiple styles. For instance, disabled or not, some people feel more spiritual in environments with minimal sensory inputs: stillness, silence, dimness. Others feel more spiritual in environments filled with noise and color and movement. For some, sitting quietly and listening carefully to a sermon is most impactful. Others find it incredibly difficult to pay attention without moving or engaging multiple senses. And most people's preferences change depending on their circumstances. A deeper truth is that neurodivergence gives people different ways of accessing and processing their spiritual feelings, yielding insights that enrich communities in which people are encouraged to learn from each other's spiritual journeys.

Rev. Jennifer DeBusk Alviar: I find myself at a crossroads. My core theological struggle is this: I experience a disconnect between my ministry and my disability. To help embody and discern this struggle on a kinesthetic level, I hold two stones in my hand. One for gratitude. The other for grief.

In my vocation as an ordained, Unitarian Universalist community minister, I am grateful that our faith tradition is not sealed in stone with infallible doctrine, dogma, and creed. We believe that revelation is ever unfolding. We remain open to change and transformation. We embrace a spirit of healing, wholeness, and liberation. We invite a sacred space for radical inclusion and hospitality in dismantling systems of oppression. This, indeed, is my stone of gratitude for our progressive movement.

My stone of grief is that our worship arts in church settings do not align well with my brain and body. For example, our Unitarian Universalist worship structure is highly verbal. As someone who struggles with language around information processing, I find this format challenging.

I experience an ache and longing for a more embodied expression of soulful, spiritual practices that affirm a multisensory approach to worship. How might we reimagine the worship arts in church in order to provide greater accessibility for people with apparent and non-apparent disabilities alike?

In 1977, I survived a life-threatening brain hemorrhage as a six-year-old child. The bursting of blood vessels left me temporarily voiceless and silent. In the months following my brain surgery, I regained my speech. Yet I noticed a marked difference in how I accessed my words. I didn't "think" my way into speech by gathering ideas in my head. Instead, I "felt" my way into speech through embodied movement grounded in the natural world.

I used visual cues and sensory touch to process what I could see and feel, but couldn't name. Over time, connecting my body with the natural world enabled me to translate images into words for verbal expression. This is the multisensory process in which I ultimately developed as a writer, preacher, and retreat facilitator. A somatic approach to living, learning, and leading.

When congregations are open to different modalities of worship and serious about affirming the individual search for truth and meaning, Unitarian Universalism can be one of the few religious spaces that honor the real intersection between neurodiversity

and spiritual understanding, providing a true home for many who have struggled elsewhere.

Rev. Tandi Rogers: I have superpowers. I am quick to forgive and forget. I have impulse control challenges that can be interpreted as boundless, enthusiastic love. That's what it feels like to me. I'm extremely creative and curious. I'm made for storytelling. I make connections, see possibilities that other people don't see. I don't have a filter that neurotypical people seem to have. It makes me thinly veiled, so God is extremely accessible to me. I don't have a neurotypical concept of time. Kairos time is my prime orientation; radical presence is my constant.

So when the doctor who gave me long hours of assessment asked with wonder what I did for a living, it made sense given my particular constellation of executive functioning challenges that I am a religious educator, teacher, and spiritual director. My classrooms are chaotic, nonlinear, and wonder-filled.

I asked my doctor what people like me usually do for a living. He shook his head and said, with tears in his eyes, "They are either in prison or dead." It was like a punch to the gut. I should have already known that, but it hadn't sunk in that it applied to me. Most of the kids I taught earlier in my life had FASD [fetal alcohol spectrum disorders] and half of them are either dead or incarcerated. There is a piece of my heart that is in constant grief over that.

I've been blessed with many supervisors and teammates who knew I was a little different (even without the official assessment). They played to my strengths and made sure I had support for things I just couldn't do. On my "off" days, we slowed down to the speed of trust and recuperation. We learned the language of spoon therapy. We shared spiritual practices. We spent time creating a team culture in which I knew I belonged.

Kate Ryan: I have always loved church. I loved the pews, the little enclosed spaces. I loved the hymns, the rituals, and the candles, the feeling of being together in an age-old community, the idea that there was something out there that could help me, no matter how bad things got. As I grew older, however, I came to realize that much of Christian theology just didn't make sense to me. I wanted logical proof of God before I believed in him. I wanted something concrete, ideally in a scholarly journal with multiple references. Unfortunately, the Christian churches that I tried never offered these things. Luckily for me, Unitarian Universalism did.

In Unitarian Universalism, I finally found the logical explanations that my autistic brain craved, as well as the hymns and community that fed my soul, whatever my soul was. Unitarian Universalism was absolutely fine with the fact that I didn't believe in God. Many of them were also atheists. Unitarian Universalists didn't ask me to make a pledge or believe in miracles, they only asked that I believe in the Principles. The Principles made wonderful, factual sense to me. So it was that in my mid-twenties I joined a local UU congregation and threw myself into being a full participant in the community. At this church, I found not only kindred spirits, but lasting friendships that have sustained me for over a decade. I found people who really did accept me for who I was, who valued what I could contribute, who helped me figure things out. I was and am at home there.

Unitarian Universalism is my religion. No other religion makes logical sense to me, because I do not just think there is no God. I know there is no God. I'm not agnostic. I'm atheist, and this lack of doubt means that I will not be fully welcomed anywhere else. The things that I learn at church about social justice and the church's idea of pressing for the rights of marginalized people keep me connected and engaged. If it were not for my church, I would not understand so many issues and so many things going on in the world. If it were not for church, I would not have so many friends. Heck, if it were not for church, I would never have figured out that I was queer!

Spirituality and Mental Health

There is also a lot of misunderstanding about the spirituality of people with mental health issues, which are often considered suspect and not treated with care and respect.

Rev. Katie Norris: My faith and call to ministry were often in question, which was very painful. People asked repeatedly throughout my ministerial formation process if I was becoming a minister because it was a calling or hyper-religiosity from bipolar disorder.

That's an interesting assumption about what spirituality and faith mean for those of us who have mental illness. Why would my deep faith be "fake," i.e., hyper-religiosity, when someone without a diagnosis is not questioned about their faith at all? It becomes more risky to talk about how you practice your faith when people believe it is not real. It was much more acceptable to talk about my faith in reason and science, which we tend to value highly in Unitarian Universalism, than my spiritual practices around tarot and my connection to the Virgin Mary that has remained with me since my Catholic childhood.

It has also been interesting to recently find out that I was misdiagnosed as bipolar for twenty-one years and I am autistic. Would my call to ministry have been questioned as being hyper-religiosity had I had the correct diagnosis back then?

Rev. Barbara Meyers: As a result of my therapy and exposure to other people hospitalized for mental illness, I had a revelation that each person is special and unique, special because of, not in spite of, their differences from the "ideal." This revelation took the form of seeing halos around the heads of some "insignificant" people. I felt this realization at the depths of my soul, and it can still bring me to tears. And I realized that I am a special person too. This was a completely different way of looking at the world—I didn't have to be perfect, and neither did anyone else!

HELPING WELL

On an interpersonal level, many non-disabled people feel anxious about whether and how to offer to help disabled people, which can lead to avoidance and isolation. We hope that offering some guidelines here will help. It's better to learn more about how disabled people experience help than to not do anything for fear of getting it wrong.

Bodily Autonomy and Personal Space

Many of the ways in which non-disabled people attempt to help disabled people violate their bodily autonomy and personal boundaries. No one should be touched, for instance, unless they have consented to it. Often disabled people are expected to be grateful for a stranger's offer to carry them or for having someone grab their elbow to help them navigate uneven terrain or a busy street. For people with certain disabilities, such as autism, physical touch is particularly uncomfortable.

Assistive devices and service animals should be treated with the same consideration for the person's autonomy and personal space. Taking away a rollator or walker and placing it out of its user's reach during a worship service, for example, takes away the person's freedom of movement, making them dependent on others to bring it back. Congregations should be familiar with how to treat service animals so that both they and their handlers are safe and comfortable. Discussion of service animals on page 50.)

Offering Help

If you notice a disabled person struggling with something like opening a door, maneuvering around an obstacle, or crossing the street, it is an act of kindness to offer to help without their having to ask you. That doesn't mean rushing in to do whatever it is you think they need! It means asking them if they would like some assistance. And even this well-meaning gesture needs thinking through. Before offering assistance, consider whether you would offer the same help to anyone else, like a person whose arms are full. Reflect on your own experiences and ask yourself if you would like it if you were in their place. If being in this position would make you feel vulnerable, what could be done so that in the future you would not feel this way? These questions shift the focus from individual acts of aid to the broader issue of accessibility. Instead of trying to help individual disabled people overcome barriers, the emphasis should be on removing the barriers altogether. A more equitable world prioritizes dismantling obstacles so that disabled people are not perpetually forced to navigate systems that exclude or marginalize them.

In general, it's better to offer a specific form of help (without assuming that you're right about what's needed) than to make a general offer. It's common to invite people to "reach out if there's anything you need." While this may feel like a thoughtful gesture, it can come across as vague or insincere. Such an offer places the burden on the other person to figure out what kind of help they need and to make the request, which can be overwhelming, especially for someone who has only recently become disabled and who may themselves still be unsure what challenges they face and how they can best meet them. Instead, making a specific offer, such as bringing a meal, running errands, or helping with transportation, provides clarity and shows genuine intention. This approach gives the person the opportunity to accept, decline, or adjust the offer to suit their needs, fostering meaningful support without adding unnecessary pressure. Interacting with disabled people beyond their disability and getting to know them means that, over time, you will become more familiar with what kinds of help the person welcomes and can offer help grounded in your relationship with them and your understanding of their unique personality and needs.

Pastoral Care

Providing pastoral care to people who have issues that sometimes intersect with disability, such as economic instability, housing problems, isolation, and hospitalization, can be a challenge for a congregation because of the magnitude of the need. Possible responses include encouraging members to visit people who are hospitalized or isolated, offering formal training in the pastoral care involved in such visits, developing a formal companioning program,[12] or developing a comprehensive list of community services to which people can be referred.

Some disabled people have limited personal support networks, or even none at all. The isolation that can accompany disability intensifies the need for pastoral care.

Katherine Rubie: There have been several times when I have been sick from chemotherapy and could have benefited from someone coming to help, but found there was just very little help available.

12 For more information on companionship, see Pathways to Promise: pathways2promise.org/companionship.

One or two people bringing a meal once a week was helpful but just not enough. Either there is not a desire to help or there is not capacity to do it. I'm not sure which one it is. But I was really struggling because I was taking care of myself. On my sickest days, I'd be lying in bed so sick I couldn't even get out of bed, and I'd lay there for hours and have no food, no drink, no nothing because I didn't have the assistance that I needed. I've come home from surgery twice and I've been on my own there too. I'm not allowed to bend over, nor allowed to pick things up, or a variety of other things that would jeopardize what had been accomplished during surgery. Recovery is a lengthy process, taking several months. Having somebody come in and help do things like sweep or mop the floor or do the dishes would have been helpful too. But I was told that this doesn't exist in terms of the kind of help that is offered.

Kelly Riedesel: There are some things that church members have done that have been particularly helpful for me. A couple of people have done incredibly powerful work with me. There's one very special friend who started off as a pastoral care coordinator with me ten years ago and remained a dear friend. Even though she doesn't specifically do that kind of work in the congregation anymore, she still takes me out for lunch and genuinely wants to know how I'm doing. Innumerable times, she has helped me in different ways after surgeries or driving me to a medical appointment. She even drove my son back from an out-of-town hospital that I had to go to for surgery so he could be with his aunt and not have to see me struggling from the pain immediately after the surgery.

Another time I needed and received help from church when I had to apply for social security disability. The lawyer had asked for personal letters from people in my life to help the judge understand my case, and our assistant minister at the time wrote one of those letters to the judge. It was so heartfelt, honest, and insightful. It made me cry because I felt so seen and understood at a time when it felt like my life was falling apart piece by piece. The support of that letter and others was a precious gift.

Caregivers and family members of disabled people need support as well. They need respite and someone who will listen empathetically to their stories. And they also sometimes need to just have fun and connect with others outside of their home. It is good practice to ask what they need and follow their lead.

When a person needs a lot of pastoral care and practical assistance over time, there is a tendency for the willingness to help to fade, particularly if a person keeps finding themselves in the same crisis repeatedly or if all of the help is being provided by only a few people.

In many congregations, the minister is seen as the sole person responsible for offering pastoral care. But the congregation as a whole should be aware of the needs of its members. Pastoral care should be a collective effort, allowing everyone, including disabled congregants, to contribute to one another's well-being.

Offering support to others can be deeply personal. First of all, It's important to know your limits. If you are uncertain of what to do in a challenging situation, deferring to a minister or other professional can be an act of self-compassion. It's also helpful to know a lot about your fellow pastoral care providers. When a challenging need arises, knowing what their backgrounds, strengths, and comfort levels with such needs are can help you know who to turn to.

Always listen deeply, and keep confidentiality except in emergencies. If someone indicates that they intend to harm someone else or themselves, or gives you reason to believe that someone, especially a child or elder, is being abused, share this with a supervising caregiver, your minister, or appropriate authorities. Know whether your role makes you a mandated reporter in your jurisdiction.

Don't underestimate the gift of being a caring presence.

Rev. Phoenix Bell-Shelton Biggs: We all have our journey, the path we take toward or away from healing. And for me, that path led me away from healing for quite a while. At my lowest points, I did not know what to do or if I wanted to do it anymore. Thoughts of suicide seemed like a friend; I thought self-harm helped ease pain. But they only hid the real pain; they were the mask, the denial, the fear, the lies I was beginning to believe about myself sneaking in. Lies that told me I was not loved or worthy. I fell victim to my mind and became a prisoner of my mind. Yet I am here today, so something must have changed.

I have answered a call to ministry because I want to be a part of others' healing and see the Unitarian Universalist faith as a powerful tool in healing when led correctly, bravely, and with love.

I had one such moment as a summer chaplain last summer, when I was called into the room of a young trans man. As the visit ended, he looked at me and said, "You get it, don't you?"

Rev. Barbara Meyers: Once, during my ministerial internship, a woman came up to me during the hustle and bustle before the Sunday service. I knew she struggled with anxiety; now, in great distress, she told me how anxious she was and that she didn't know what to do. She was frantic, and I didn't know what I could do for her. At a loss, I suggested that we get out of the busy hallway and go together to a nearby room. I sat with her there, holding her hand in silence, and thinking, "What can I do? What can I do?" After a couple of minutes, she turned to me and said, "I feel so much better just being here with you." I was amazed to realize that just by being present with her, caring about her, I had helped her, that my presence in and of itself was a gift, and her acknowledging it was a gift to me.

If you are offering pastoral care to a disabled person, know the difference between compassion and ableism, between being a true friend and becoming a "savior" by thinking you know what the person needs. And be wary of making judgments about others' circumstances. Often disabled people are accused of mismanaging their own lives without recognition of the ways in which an ableist society creates challenges and obstacles that lead to crises.

Katherine Rubie: A good deal of my time is spent in a search for housing. Because I am a disabled veteran and dependent on Uncle Sam for an income and a housing voucher, I am not able to just pick up and move out or live anywhere I want to, like most people can. And that's frustrating too. Trying to find housing in a market that is extremely limited in affordable housing seems to consume my time.

I became a member of the congregation in 2008. I have had to move around a lot because every time the rent went up, I couldn't afford it and was forced to find a cheaper place. I feel that often the congregation was unconcerned about my situation or I was driving people away because the few people that helped by packing or moving boxes began dwindling away. I have assumed they got tired of helping because they kept seeing the same thing over and over again, with no change or stability, and then I finally became homeless.

As a member of a congregation where I feel that we're supposed to be helping each other grow and fully participate, I cannot help but feel that I'm being shunned by the congregation. It has made me want to isolate myself several times over the years.

It is a common practice in most Unitarian Universalist faith communities to offer many forms of pastoral care to people and families coping with physical illness or injury. But all too often, mental illness goes unseen and unattended to. Mental and emotional illnesses are sometimes called "no casserole diseases" because people don't bring casseroles to families who have a member hospitalized for mental or emotional problems. Discomfort, unexamined assumptions, and cultural norms isolate people and families who are in desperate need of community support.

Accomplices: How to Be a Darn Good Ally

We use the term *accomplices* instead of *allies* to signify people who don't just talk about supporting disabled people; they take action to change systems and knock down barriers. All disability accomplices must be willing to speak up when they see examples of oppression. They must actively challenge ableist assumptions and address resistance to change, especially in everyday interactions such as ableist language.

Timing is everything in shifting attitudes, and addressing ableism in the moment gives people an opportunity to reflect and learn while memories are fresh, course correction is possible, and the person who has called attention to ableism is less likely to be perceived as overreacting than they might be if they brought up the topic long after the moment had passed. It isn't necessary to be critical or confrontational when someone says or does something ableist; a calm, respectful approach can be more powerful. For example, suggesting alternative language or explaining why a comment might be problematic can help build awareness and encourage others to think more critically about how they speak about disabled people. By taking action in these small but meaningful ways, allies can contribute to a more inclusive environment and help dismantle the biases in our congregations. Even if the person you are trying to educate reacts badly, you never know who might be listening. Someone who overheard the interaction may feel better equipped to address a similar situation themselves. Or perhaps the person who reacted badly on the spot will have time to reflect and course-correct in the future.

Gale Callaghan: So why not give up? Why not stop going to Sunday services and say, "It isn't for me"? The simple answer is because it is for me. The community I've found in Unitarian Universalism is unlike any place I've been before. When someone talks down to me or speaks over me, there are always five more people calling me back in. I know I'm wanted because of the consistent behavior of other members of the community.

Rev. Barbara Meyers: In large meetings, I can't hear unless people use a mic. I remember being in a large meeting room where someone started to speak without using the mic. A couple of hearing people said, "Use the mic." I was so relieved and grateful to them.

Lisa Ferris: The most important reason I stayed so long and kept trying was that Dwight and I had champions in the congregation. There were a few people who always advocated for us and tried to make things work for us. These were both congregants and staff. Our biggest champion in our early UU days was the religious education director, Sara Cloe. If not for Sara, we would not have lasted more than maybe a few months. But Sara helped advocate for an assistive listening device for me and other hard of hearing folks, she advocated for the parish house to have a ramp, and she advocated for rides for us to off-grounds activities that we couldn't get to on our own. She even advocated for a covenant group to be made to help specifically include us and arranged childcare. We made friends in that group that I still care about and keep in touch with to this day. It was one of the lasting gifts that came out of our UU experience.

Kate Ryan: There are times when I cannot speak for myself and need others to do so for me. There are times when I do not have a voice or a way to communicate but I still need access. Everyone needs access, and everyone deserves access.

One of the kindest things that you can do to support disabled people is to advocate for them whether they are in the room or not. This relieves the disabled person of the necessity of always being the one to request an accommodation and lets them know that the people in the organization are looking out for their interests. Of course, be mindful that if you are advocating for a specific person's access needs, that you first learn what they are and ask that person if they would like help with advocacy.

Maria Zuccarello: In my daily life, my worth is validated when someone hears my life story or values my needs in regard to my disability in such a way that they incorporate what they learned about my disability into their worldview so that they see and interact with the world more through my lens—whether I am there or not.

No one wants to think of themselves as an oppressor; yet we oppress others when we do nothing to counter their oppression. We can all act today and contribute to the changes disabled people need in our communities, in our nation, and in our world.

Anonymous: I'm a lobbyist, and I'm also a sandwich maker and a meals-on-wheels volunteer. If you want to improve community health, and if you want to encourage sustainability and resilience, it's important to be involved on several levels of activity. Improve access to essential services. The climate crisis is a problem that should be mentioned. People have been left during hurricanes and ignored during heat waves. There's a need for multicultural, multifaith, and multigenerational ministry, and it's needed in the here and now.

Try to understand what's happening in the present moment. The economy is changing, the technology is changing, and even the weather is changing. At the moment, average life expectancy is declining in the United States, and the decline has something to do with the social determinants of health. People want to live in a better way, in healthy communities where neighbors care about each other. In this new reality, it's the disability justice people who will provide much of the insight and much of the leadership.

Acceptance alone is not enough; it is imperative that we take intentional steps to build a culture of belonging and equity. Our shared values, with love at the center, call us to build diverse, multicultural beloved communities where everyone feels welcome and has the opportunity to thrive. To live out these values, we must move beyond the walls of our congregations and form meaningful partnerships with social organizations that advocate for and support disabled people, especially ones run by disabled people themselves. By collaborating with these groups, we can amplify their efforts to promote accessibility, inclusion, and justice for disabled people across all aspects of society. This commitment aligns with our moral and spiritual obligation to dismantle barriers and create a world where all people can fully participate and flourish.

INTERSECTIONALITY

By now we hope you're well attuned to how important it is to engage with disabled people as their whole selves, not just around their disability. In the disability justice context, this means also being curious, mindful, and empathetic about how ableism intersects with other aspects of a person's identity to shape their lived experience. When we create access and actively welcome and include disabled people in our communities, with their focus on social justice, we also give them the space to explore and share in community all the parts of themselves and how they connect.

Lisa Holcomb: I love how Unitarian Universalists not only fight for the rights of people who are disabled but understand and discuss the nuances between the disability rights movement and the newer disability justice movement. They see that the older movement still excludes people of color and people with different sexual or gender identities and are working to support the newer movement, which aims to help even more people than the older one did.

Imari S. Nuyen-Kariotis: I am hopeful that the disability rights movement will continue to grow and evolve into the disability justice movement. The disability justice movement is a movement that recognizes that disability is not just a medical condition but also a social construct. The disability justice movement is working to create a society where disabled people are valued and respected. I believe that the disability justice movement has the potential to create a more just and equitable world for all people.

My intersectional framework is important to me because it helps me to understand the different ways that my identities intersect and impact my experiences. As a BIPOC person with disabilities, I face multiple layers of oppression. I am often stereotyped and discriminated against because of my race, my disability, or both. My intersectional framework helps me to see the ways that these different forms of oppression are connected, and it gives me the tools to fight back against them.

UU congregations can help in the disability justice movement by educating themselves about disability. This includes learning not only about different disabilities but also about the history and culture of the disability community and UU history around disability.

UU congregations can also become allies to the disability community. This means advocating for the rights of people with disabilities and working to create a more inclusive society. Most of all, support UU disability-led organizations.

Dana Snyder-Grant: At a bimonthly gathering of the pastoral care choir, a few of us engaged in a conversation about disability within the congregation. My presence and involvement with the group gave this concept more traction. Our director of music ministry introduced the concept of collective liberation. It seems that increased awareness of systems of oppression combined with our awareness of radical inclusion can only increase our awareness of and responsiveness to disability within our congregation. We felt hopeful and full of possibility. I came home and began reading more, understanding that my struggle or oppression is your struggle and vice versa.

Kaden Colton: I taught a couple different RE classes while I attended the larger UU congregation. I came out as transgender and queer around the same time I was cofacilitating an RE class. The changing of names and pronouns was difficult for myself and others. I experienced quite a bit of people calling me by the wrong name and pronouns when I interacted with them during the social hour after service.

I stopped attending services at this particular UU congregation for a couple years because I had a difficult time with the ableism and transphobia. I didn't want to have to deal with being continuously misgendered during the social hour after the service or not having the same access to printed material as everyone else that I dealt with constantly. I liked the people I met through the congregation, but I needed some separation. I was also feeling burned out around the same time due to being the only visibly disabled person going through the atmospheric sciences program at the University of Utah.

I ended up attending South Valley Unitarian Universalist Society after I felt ready to rejoin a congregation. I can still remember my first visit to this congregation. It was during the winter. I researched how to get to this particular congregation via the public transportation system that exists within the Salt Lake City area the day prior. I knew which bus to get on, where the stops were to get on and off the bus, and how to navigate to and from them.

The bus I needed would be about a block from the building. I went through with my plan to attend the service. I turned off the sidewalk next to the street and onto the pathway up to the front entrance of the congregation. The first thing I could see made me pause for a moment. Could this congregation be my spiritual home? A giant rainbow flag hung directly above the front doors. This flag was large enough for me to see from about twenty feet away. I felt welcome, even before I crossed the threshold. I walked into the building and was greeted by some people in the foyer. I was even welcomed by the minister personally. One of the people who worked in the office asked if I wanted to be a part of a group of people receiving the hymns for the upcoming Sunday's service in an electronic format that was accessible to screen reader users. I felt like I need not worry as much about being included as a trans and blind person with a UU congregation. This feeling of inclusion stuck with me while I attended South Valley and even when I moved to Minnesota at the end of January of 2020.

Cathy Welburn: During the Middle Ages, a sanctuary knocker was posted on the outer door of churches throughout England. According to church law, a fugitive need only touch the knocker to be free from arrest and find a safe haven while appealing their case.

On November 30, 1993, Mauricio Romero, age thirty-five, failed to show up at the Calgary airport to be deported to El Salvador. He had been denied refugee status and lost several appeals on compassionate grounds due to his newly diagnosed medical condition of schizophrenia. An arrest warrant was issued, and he went into hiding. Several churches, spearheaded by lawyer Claire McMordie of Scarborough United Church, learned of this and approached the Calgary Unitarian Church to provide sanctuary. While sanctuary has had no legal standing since Reformation times, it has been frequently invoked symbolically by congregations in North America. Granting sanctuary focuses attention on moral and humanitarian issues. Authorities do not like to take people from sanctuaries. Unitarians have a history of offering refuge to immigrants and displaced people in need of a place of safety since the Unitarian Service Committee was first organized in 1945.

Mauricio's family had fled El Salvador in the 1980s, fearing the violence that killed so many resisting the authoritarian regime backed by the United States. His parents and several brothers had already settled in Calgary and become citizens. They were prepared to support him. Mauricio had fled, with two older brothers, to Nicaragua, where they worked for several years and his brothers were killed by death squads. Mauricio won a scholarship to Bulgaria from the Communist Party in El Salvador, where he studied engineering until the Eastern Communist Bloc collapsed. He was deported back to El Salvador in 1991, but got off the plane in Newfoundland, where it had stopped for refueling. After joining his family in Calgary, he spent years applying for refugee status because of the danger awaiting him in El Salvador.

Unitarian minister Rev. Josiah Bartlett stated in 1993 the simple moral proposition that when a person's life is threatened, the public conscience needs to be very clear before sending him, with no family to receive him, to a place known to regard him as a possible "disappeared" rather than giving him a home.

The Calgary church quickly agreed to provide sanctuary, giving time for immigration authorities to reconsider the case. With remarkable speed, an ad hoc committee of several churches welcomed Mauricio into a home in the church basement.

Supporters raised money. Volunteers taught Mauricio English. His family banded together to fix up the living arrangements and support Mauricio in every way. His mother and father slept over. His mother basically ran a short-order café where people gathered to chat with the family. Even the youth group would walk with him in the enclosed garden space and play games with him. "It was a very sick time for me," says Mauricio, remembering thirty years later. "But I had been supported by doctors who were so good to me. They gave me free medication and helped me understand my schizophrenia. They reached out to me and never gave up. People came to play music and sing. People came to offer me jobs when I got out. They signed petitions for my cause. Then, in the church, I began to feel better, especially with my parents there." The Romero family became part of our church family. Volunteers were present for four shifts a day. A twenty-four-hour vigil was set up so he was never alone. The church was never locked. Authorities were free to enter at any time.

Protests began outside the federal Hays Building in Calgary as Christmas approached, bringing media attention to the case. Protesters carried signs stating, "Give him a chance" or "Keep the family together" and kept a twelve-day vigil until Christmas. The church had to find new ways to carry on its normal business as well as respond to the media. A new phone line was installed, with someone responsible for answering calls. Reaction of the congregation was affirmative even though the church became a focal point for people who were not supportive, some even threatening. People came to talk, argue, and question what was happening in our church. However, with many people of all faiths coming into the building, a new year began and we settled into a routine. It became a very strengthening time for us as individuals and as a congregation, as we hoped to spur better immigration procedures for those who came to Canada.

Mauricio's lawyer, Michael Greene, and an ad hoc committee who advocated for him with immigration authorities reasoned that four siblings and parents, all of whom had fled El Salvador, were Canadian citizens and taxpayers willing to support him. With his medical condition, he was better off with family and treatments in Canada. He had no family in El Salvador. Two of his brothers had already been slain. Death squad activity had increased recently with the signing of the peace accord, and Mauricio was a prime target for persecution.

On May 25, 1994, after six months of confinement in quarters never intended for living, Mauricio, his faithful parents with him throughout, was granted a ministerial permit to remain in Canada for five years. After six months spent learning English, playing cards, and praying he wouldn't be deported, he stepped out of the Unitarian church.

The permit came with stringent conditions—mainly that Mauricio wouldn't become a drain on the medical or welfare system. Critics feared that he would not be able to overcome his illness.

"Eight years later, he hasn't cost Canada a dime," Mauricio's lawyer reported. The reason: a large support network and the kindness of two doctors who donated time and medication for his treatment. Mauricio was eventually able to become a Canadian citizen. "I worked in surveying and seismic for many years," he recalls, "sometimes taking me far from home. I had many jobs, anything I could get. Finally, I found a job as a landscaper in Calgary near my family. I worked there for twenty years before retiring. "I loved to take my mother out to restaurants," he says, smiling broadly. "I was a good son. I was happy to help my mother after all she did for me."

Mauricio's time in the sanctuary at the Calgary church sparked nationwide support for his case. Rev. Bartlett said, "These months of sanctuary have affirmed for all Canadians the privileges we have in a sadly inhumane world. We have learned much about advocacy. We have allies, often unexpected allies, in any good cause. We don't have to go it alone."

LESSONS FROM THE PANDEMIC

For any group of people learning about equity and inclusion, progress is largely gradual and nonlinear. We have false starts, our will to change falls short of what we know we should do, we encounter resistance, and we give other things priority. But sometimes events beyond our control crystallize what's important and we move forward with greater focus and determination. The beginning of the COVID pandemic was one of those times.[13] When UU congregations had no choice but to take seriously questions of access and inclusion in the face of a disease that killed, sickened, and disabled millions of people, we did—not perfectly, and not without difficulty, but with real positive impact that may last and propel further growth. Here is some of what we learned, together.

Motivation makes the impossible possible. During the pandemic, many congregations discovered that they could do online worship well, something that many of them had rejected as impossible when it was requested as an accommodation for disabled and isolated people. When everyone needed that

13 Although the World Health Organization declared COVID-19 no longer a global emergency in May 2023, the virus is still a part of everyday life for many people. It continues to spread and change, and its impact remains serious—especially for those with Long COVID, weakened immune systems, or limited access to healthcare. Many still face ongoing illness, strict isolation, or long-term symptoms like fatigue and brain fog. While much of society has moved on, COVID continues to cause deaths, strain healthcare systems, and disrupt lives. The pandemic is not over for everyone; it has shifted into a lasting reality that affects people in unequal ways.

accommodation, it became possible. We might keep this in mind when future "impossible" accommodations are requested.

Equity means acknowledging differences in vulnerability. The pandemic made clear that not everyone has the same level of access to safety, resources, and social connection. For non-disabled people, masking, social distancing, rarely leaving home, and other precautions against disease were unfamiliar and even shocking; but for some disabled people, especially immunocompromised people, they were already familiar aspects of everyday life. When the public health emergency was declared over in 2023, many people cheered for a "return to normal." What was lost in the celebration was a recognition that what non-disabled people considered normal was a level of access and opportunity that many disabled people did not enjoy until shutdowns forced society to create new means of access. The rhetoric of celebrating normalcy was deeply traumatizing to those for whom the end of the shutdowns meant loss. Many disabled people had experienced the world as more equitable when a majority had been concerned with safety and accessibility, and when restricting travel and remaining at home had been unremarkable, even sometimes mandated. It took the pandemic to make some non-disabled people recognize that immunocompromised people require special care and consideration just to survive. It's important to carry forward the lessons we learned in those years about protecting, caring for, and maintaining connection with each other.

We are truly interdependent. Affirming interdependence has long been a Unitarian Universalist value, but the pandemic made interdependence feel real to many of us in new ways. We were called to help each other when services we were used to were unavailable, when low-paid workers were called essential and required to face risks that others could avoid, when we had to work together to find ways to work and worship remotely, and especially when we had to keep each other safe from contagion.

Having to mask and isolate themselves gave non-disabled people a chance to experience a little of what many disabled people live with every day. So did having to find alternative ways to do things in a world built for a different way of being. The adaptability that non-disabled people had to learn in order to work, maintain relationships, and provide for their basic needs during the shutdown is nothing new to the disability community.

Helen Armstrong: As a disabled woman, living during COVID lockdowns felt like one more layer of familiar isolation. My congregation, Neighbourhood Unitarian Universalist Congregation, kept me connected during the mass-disabling pandemic. I readily embraced the move to online services. I am immunocompromised and was grateful to be able to stay home and feel safe. Even now, I know that if I feel unwell, I can participate with others from my home. Online access is a disability accommodation and a big step forward for our congregation. It also helps those who live far away. Our challenge now is to go further with disability access.

As I write this, my city, Toronto, is enveloped in a haze of wildfire smoke from fires in the north. My asthma is worsening, and I feel despair that I am isolated. Knowing that I may remain homebound is frightening, but my UU faith partly sustains me, as does the web of connections with my UU community. This need for adapted engagement will be more important as we continue to experience escalating climate chaos.

Diana C. Archibald: It was and still is horrifying and heartbreaking to see the effects of the pandemic, a global catastrophe. The way we came together using technology, however, in a way put everyone in the same boat. None of us were going to the building. But we were going to church.

When I was a teenager, I belonged to an evangelical church that had been fundraising for years to construct their own building so we could leave the rented space where we worshiped and settle into our own space. When a fire consumed the entire church, including the newly installed pipe organ, just a few weeks before we were scheduled to open, the pastor told the reporter at the scene, "Our church has not been destroyed—only our building. The church is us. And we are still present for each other."

During lockdown, this memory floated back to me. The church is us. While I understand that for some the pandemic brought loneliness and isolation, in many ways I felt a sense of equity and camaraderie that I had not experienced for quite some time. But now almost everyone seems to believe COVID-19 is no longer a concern. It is business as usual now, and "let's get back to normal."

Despite the US government declaring an end to the public health emergency, the only thing that has ended is government support for those in need due to this catastrophe. Those of us who are vulnerable know that it is not over: every four minutes, someone dies from this disease, and 16 million Americans have long COVID. Those hardest hit are the elderly, the disabled, and the chronically ill. For us, the emergency remains. For everyone, the danger remains: new variants that surpass all protections have a strong chance of emerging in the coming months and years. Public health funding cuts increase the likelihood that future pandemics will wreak havoc.

L. A. Wright: Few people questioned who was not in the sanctuary or the meeting room or the potluck social. When COVID pushed everyone into isolation, things changed. Now that we know better, we need to heed the words of Maya Angelou: "Do the best you can until you know better. Then when you know better, do better."

Neva Allen: With the number of people who have died from COVID, it's hard for me to say this, but it actually was a blessing in disguise for me. My church decided they would put their services on Zoom and purchased the technology necessary to do so. Because of their decision, for the first time, I have felt like I have been fully able to participate. I was on the Social Action Committee for a time; I attended the Seasoned Souls group, and I help the minister by hosting the Thursday Connections meetings on Zoom that have been made by my church. Even though I'm not able to physically attend, I feel like I'm actually part of the church more than I have at any other time. I have gotten to know most of the people in the church more intimately through these meetings, and I will be forever grateful to my minister for understanding my situation as well as those of others when it comes to the ability to physically attend church. Because of her understanding and her promotion to the church community about the importance of the technology necessary to continue having church during COVID, I think everyone has become more acutely aware of what it means to be a truly inclusive church.

Having the technology and using Zoom has allowed those like me to attend, but also members who have moved away or are traveling, and new people who want to learn more about the church.

I had felt in my heart what I had been asking for many years would eventually come to pass. I am just sorry it took the pandemic to happen before it did.

HOPE FOR THE FUTURE

Most of the people who sent in stories for this book mentioned that in addition to the barriers they have faced, they have also experienced beautiful and compassionate treatment by some congregants and leaders. They name simple presence and listening, bringing food, giving rides, sending cards, and asking what would be helpful for them at home, in Sunday service, or in other community events and finding a way to provide it. They talk about the sincere gratitude that they feel and how it lasts for years. Some of them told us stories of the grace that came to them when they gained a new understanding of theology that includes disabled people, a new way to worship that works for them, a new understanding of disability justice, and a deep realization that they are worthy people with inherent dignity. In some cases, this realization changed their lives.

Rev. Keith Kron: Our understandings will evolve and change. Our sense of justice will germinate. Our commitment to live our Unitarian Universalist values will deepen. And we will continue to work beyond the stereotypes, beyond the not being seen or seen as only a single story and continue to figure out how to be together and know the whole human beings in front of us living lives filled with hope and joy and difficulty as best they can, as best we can. There are so many great people we have not met and do not know.

Lisa Holcomb: One thing I love about Unitarian Universalism as a whole is its commitment to social justice. Many years ago, I belonged to a different church that was also committed to social justice, and when I left that church home for our move to another city, I hadn't realized what an unusual situation that was. Coming to the Unitarian Universalists was like coming home, in that respect. Being able to join with other people in a church setting who are actually concerned about the rights of others who are not necessarily like themselves is amazing. Most churches I've attended don't even have a system in place to have dialogues about social justice, much less an ongoing history of siding with the oppressed in our country and helping them get their rights like Unitarian Universalism does.

Rev. Katie Norris: You may be wondering why I stayed, or even became a minister. That's a good question. I actually took a break from church and public community ministry for a while, to be honest. However, the inherent worth and dignity of every person is a core of our faith that I held on to. That and covenant. When we see people included in ways that work for them, in everyday church life, we know we are welcome, and that changes everything.

Rev. Amanda Schuber: Today, as I navigate my own ministry, I'm still faced with the frustration of having to teach others to think with an accessibility lens. I still face the assumptions and the desire of others to save me or place me in a bubble. I still feel the lack of direct conversation about the intersections of oppressed identity. Despite the familiarity of these realities, I've seen changes in how we, as a people of faith, see and honor the lived experiences of disabled people. And I'm hopeful. I believe in a future that centers our lives and our stories, one that believes in our realities and has room for us just as we are.

We'd like to conclude simply, with faith and hope, by saying that we are grateful to you for reading this book and for the efforts you have made and will continue to make to expand the circle of belonging ever wider in our congregations, to understand the lived realities of disabled people, and to advocate for us in the larger world. We remind you that perfection is not the goal and right where you are is always the right place to begin. No effort toward inclusion is ever wasted. You will make mistakes, and you will encounter resistance. You will sometimes have to make difficult decisions and realign priorities. But every time someone feels, whether for the first time or as a beloved reminder, that their whole self is cherished in a faith community that aligns with their heart and soul, it has a lasting impact on them, their community, and the world. The work is never done. But we join L. A. Wright in reminding you of the admonition often credited to Maya Angelou:

Do the best you can until you know better. Then when you know better, do better.

Reflection Questions

Rev. Sierra-Marie Gerfao

Introduction/Every Congregation Has Work to Do

Questions for Individual Reflection

1. What personal experiences with disability am I bringing into this book?
2. What are my hopes for what this book will offer me or my community?
3. What self-care will I practice if I experience discomfort while reading this book?

Questions for Community Reflection

1. How did we react to the idea that disability is common in Unitarian Universalist communities?
2. In what ways is it helpful to consider that aging increases the likelihood of disability, and in what ways is it unhelpful?
3. Is there work we already know we need to do in order to be more inclusive of disabled people?

Disability Basics

Questions for Individual Reflection

1. Who are the people in my life who know and accept my needs, and how has that acceptance been communicated?
2. What beliefs did I have about disability earlier in my life that I no longer believe?
3. What beliefs do I have about disability now that I did not have earlier in my life?

Questions for Community Reflection

1. What models of disability, or beliefs about disability, are reflected in how our community approaches the inclusion of disabled people?
2. Who carries responsibility for disability advocacy in our community right now?
3. Do any of the stigmas about disability described here feel familiar in our community?

Common Responses to Disabled People

Questions for Individual Reflection

1. When I think about respectful, mutual relationships in my community, what do they look and feel like?
2. What feelings arose for me as I read about each of the common responses to disabled people (inspiration, fear, pity, fixing, trivialization, distrust, etc.)?
3. When have I been called in, or when have I called someone else in, for a problematic response to disabled people, and what happened after that?

Questions for Community Reflection

1. Which of the common responses to disabled people show up most frequently in our community?

    a. using disabled people for inspiration
    b. expecting disabled people to be teachers
    c. pity
    d. conflation or overgeneralization
    e. fear and discomfort
    f. removing disabled people from view
    g. fixing
    h. judgment
    i. centering the disability instead of the person
    j. trivialization
    k. resentment and silencing
    l. distrust
    m. defensiveness

2. As a community, have we ever addressed or called people in from one of these common responses, and what happened when we did?
3. As a community, how have we fostered a culture of respect and mutuality that is inclusive of disabled people?

Accessibility and Inclusion

Questions for Individual Reflection

1. How do people in my community make their needs known?

2. When have I felt my gifts were valued in community, enough that I have been freely offered support so that I can share those gifts?
3. What experiences do I have with disability representation in my community?

Questions for Community Reflection

1. How can our community continually consult with disabled people to make improvements to accessibility and inclusion without expecting them to create the solutions or be community educators?
2. What do we know now about what we need to do next to be more accessible and inclusive, and what do we still need to know?
3. Are we in agreement with what our organizational policies say about how the needs of disabled people will be met and how ableism will be addressed?

Impacts of Ableism

Questions for Individual Reflection

1. How does ableism show up in my life?
2. What have I personally experienced or observed about the relationship between disability and isolation?
3. How do my own experiences with disillusionment in community impact how I read the stories of disillusionment in this book?

Questions for Community Reflection

1. Are there ways in which our community fosters isolation among disabled people?
2. In what ways do we practice flexibility and openness toward behaviors and needs that fall outside norms?
3. When someone in our community has an accessibility need or identifies how they can be more fully included, how many asks does it take and how long does it take for change to occur?

Meeting Spiritual Needs

Questions for Individual Reflection

1. What are my own spiritual needs?
2. How has my personal search for truth and meaning been impacted by how my brain or body works?
3. What encounters, if any, have I had with disability theology?

Questions for Community Reflection

1. What spiritual offerings does our community have for people "living in a world that isn't designed for them" and does not recognize "their full selves"?
2. What messages about disability do we communicate in our worship, teaching, and community life?
3. Is disability theology explicitly lifted up in our community?

Helping Well

Questions for Individual Reflection

1. When have I received help that was helpful, and when have I received help that was unhelpful?
2. When have I given help to others that was helpful, and when have I given help to others that was unhelpful?
3. Have I ever been forced to depend on the kindness of a stranger because an environment was not designed for all people?

Questions for Community Reflection

1. What have we done to grow our pastoral care capacity?
2. Has our community been an accomplice to disabled people?
3. When and how does our community actively engage with any disability-centered organizations?

Intersectionality

Questions for Individual Reflection

1. What do I know about the disability rights movement and what do I know about the disability justice movement?
2. Which of my own identities have come together to influence how I have read and received the stories in this book?
3. How is my liberation wrapped up in disability justice?

Questions for Community Reflection

1. Is the concept of "intersectionality" familiar to our community, and what do we know about it?
2. How does our community's work for disability justice interact with our work for other forms of justice?
3. What are our community's stories of intersectional justice work?

Lessons from the Pandemic

Questions for Individual Reflection

1. Did the pandemic change my own experiences with disability?
2. What impact has my community's ongoing responses to the pandemic had on me?
3. What impact have my own experiences with the pandemic had on my community?

Questions for Community Reflection

1. What did we used to call "impossible" in our community that we discovered was actually possible when we had the collective motivation to do it during the pandemic?
2. How have different people in our community continued to experience this phase of Covid-19 differently from one another?
3. What changes did we make together during the pandemic that have been lasting, and how did we decide which changes to stick with and which to let go?

Hope for the Future

Questions for Individual Reflection

1. What are some of the beautiful and compassionate experiences that I have had in my community?
2. What have I personally gained from reading this book?
3. Where can or does my own hope for the future come from?

Questions for Community Reflection

1. What have we learned about our community by reading this book together?
2. What changes do we want to move ahead with together after reading this book?
3. Where are the sources of hope in our community?

Glossary

Ableism—The belief that disabled people are inferior to, or worth less than, non-disabled people, and the oppression and injustice that this belief leads to.

Accessibility—The quality of being usable by or suitable for everyone, including disabled people.

Accessibility and Inclusion Ministry (AIM) Program—A credentialing program offered to Unitarian Universalist congregations from 2016 to 2022, meant to dismantle ableism and promote full inclusion of disabled people in all areas of congregational life.

Americans with Disabilities Act (ADA)—A federal civil rights law, enacted in 1990, that prohibits discrimination against disabled people in most areas of public life, including employment, education, transportation, and public spaces. Places of worship are exempt, however.

EqUUal Access—An affinity group of the UUA. Its website states, "We are disabled Unitarian Universalists, our families, friends, and allies coming together for a common purpose: To enable the full engagement of people with disabilities in Unitarian Universalist communities and the broader society" (equualaccess.org/).

Eugenics—The philosophy or practice of attempting to "improve" the human race by promoting reproduction among people considered to have desirable heritable traits and discouraging or preventing it among people considered to have undesirable ones.

Identity-First Language—Phrasing in which the disability precedes the person, such as "blind person." Compare **person-first language**. Identity-first language was born from the disability pride movement, and many disabled people prefer it to person-first language.

Inclusion—The philosophy or practice of ensuring that everyone can use the same facilities, take part in the same activities, and enjoy the same experiences, including disabled or otherwise disadvantaged people.

Microaggression—A comment or action that subtly, perhaps unintentionally or even unconsciously, reflects bigotry, prejudice, or stereotyping of an oppressed or marginalized group.

Model of Disability—A model is a way of conceptualizing disability, including its nature, origins, and implications. Models influence not only personal attitudes but legislation, institutional policies, and social practices. Many different models of disability have predominated in different times, places, and sociocultural contexts; this book discusses the medical, social, rehabilitation, charity, cultural, and biopsychosocial models (page 16).

Person-First Language—Phrasing in which the person precedes the disability, such as "person who is blind." Compare **identity-first language**. Some people with disabilities prefer person-first language.

Universal Design—The design and composition of an environment, building, product, service, etc., so that it is as accessible, understandable, and usable as possible by all people.

Surveys

Online links to fillable pdf surveys that you can download, customize, and use can be found on the EqUUal Access website at: **equualaccess.org/resources-2/congregational-disability-surveys**. The surveys to be found there are:

- What Do You Need: This survey can be used to determine what kinds of support are needed for disabled people in your congregation
- Accessibility Survey: This survey can be used to inquire about unmet disability needs
- Disability in Our Congregation: This survey can be used to identify disabled people in your congregation

We strongly recommend that you make your survey available in multiple formats, such as printed forms that can be filled out and turned in (remember to provide large-print versions) and electronic forms that can be filled out online (ensure that the website meets accessibility standards). However you choose to administer the survey, keep these tips in mind:

- Ensure that the questions are easy to understand.
- Allow sufficient time for congregants to submit their answers, and offer ways for people to submit further thoughts after the survey has officially closed.
- Know how you will tabulate and analyze the survey results and decide on your next steps. A survey is useless if it prompts no action!

Links to Resources

If you are reading this as an ebook, you will not need the following QR code or bit.ly address. Simply click the links and follow them to their corresponding documents or websites. If you are reading a copy of the printed book, you can scan the QR code or type the bit.ly address into the address bar of your web browser; this will take you to a Google doc with clickable links.

https://bit.ly/UUDisabilityLinks

Acknowledgments

We wish to acknowledge the significant input and work of Mary Benard and the Skinner House team in helping to create the format of the book and the many details involved in making it happen. We also wish to acknowledge both the people who contributed stories and those whose stories aren't in the book.

We are grateful for the work of EqUUal Access and the people who were active in the AIM program as administrators, reviewers, and teams in congregations, all of whom contributed to the wisdom that we have endeavored to impart in this book. And we are grateful for the support of the UUA in helping to fund the AIM program.